# EXPLORE

# MARRAKECH

# CONTENTS

### ARCHITECTURE

Admire the 12th-century minaret of the Koutoubia Mosque (route 1), be dazzled by the magnificent Ben Youssef Madrassa (route 2), and get lost in the labyrinthine El Bahia Palace (route 4).

# RECOMMENDED ROUTES FOR...

### ARTS AND CRAFTS

Explore the city's history at the Museum of Marrakech (route 2), visit the Dar Si Said and Maison Tiskiwin (route 4) and be dazzled by the Islamic Arts Museum in the Majorelle Garden (route 7).

### CHILDREN

As well as the evening entertainment on the Jemaa el Fna (route 1), kids will enjoy a camel ride in the Palmeraie (route 7) or a trip in a horse-drawn carriage (route 9).

### FABULOUS VIEWS

Get a bird's-eye view of the Jemaa el Fna (route 1), watch the sunset from the El Badi Palace (route 5), and admire the dramatic scenery of the great Atlas passes (routes 12, 13 and 14).

## PARKS AND GARDENS

Marrakech is renowned for its gardens, from the great Sultanic garden of the Menara (route 8) to the magical Majorelle Garden (route 7) and the lush grounds of La Mamounia hotel (route 8).

## SHOPPERS

Spreading north of the Jemaa el Fna are Marrakech's legendary souks (route 2). For chic boutiques explore the medina's Mouassine Quarter (route 3) or wander down Rue de la Liberté in Guéliz (route 6).

## SPORTING ACTIVITIES

Go horse-riding or play golf in the Palmeraie (route 7), try quad biking, kite-boarding and surfing in Essaouira (route 10) or hike up Mount Toubkal, the highest mountain in North Africa (route 12).

## STRESS RELIEF

Loosen up with a massage and scrub in the sumptuous spas and hammams of Marrakech (route 5) or lounge beside the pool at Nikki Beach in the Palmeraie (route 7).

# INTRODUCTION

An introduction to Marrakech's geography, customs and culture, plus illuminating background information on cuisine, history and what to do when you're there.

*Place des Epices*

# EXPLORE MARRAKECH

*Despite the city's continuing modernisation and ever-growing numbers of tourists, Marrakech still offers a unique and authentically Moroccan experience, set between mountain and desert at the cultural crossroads of Africa and Arabia.*

With all that Marrakech has to offer, it's difficult not to fall for the place. Accessible yet exotic, and enjoying year-round sunshine, it's also the gateway to some of Morocco's most fascinating areas, including the Atlas mountains, and has both snowy mountain peaks and Saharan sands within easy striking distance.

## DEVELOPMENT

Set on the Haouz Plain beneath the peaks of the High Atlas Mountains, Marrakech spreads red and low amid palms and olive groves. The city was founded by the Almoravids, a Berber dynasty, in 1060, at the crossroads of intercontinental trade routes linking sea and desert. For merchants and travellers it was the first great city north of the Sahara.

### The Red City

The adobe walls that the Almoravids built to enclose their settlement still form the basis of today's impressive ramparts. Extending for some 16km (10 miles) and entered by a dozen gates *(babs)*, they glow in the afternoon sun, earning Marrakech the epithet the 'Red City'.

Inside the walls is the Medina (old town), a warren of narrow, tightly packed alleyways and *derbs* (dead ends). At the heart of the medina is the great Jemaa el Fna, a large irregular-shaped square ringed by cafés and filled nightly with an extraordinary cast of snake-charmers, story-tellers, street performers, acrobats, water-sellers and Gnaoua musicians whose incessant drumming fills the night air with the hynoptic rhythms of sub-Saharan Africa.

North of the square are Marrakech's famous souks, piled high with colourful heaps of carpets, clothes, leatherwear, metalwork and many other crafts, still practised here as they have been for generations.

West of the medina is the New Town (Ville Nouvelle), founded by the French in 1912 following the creation of the French and Spanish protectorates. The contrast between Medina and New Town could hardly be greater, with the old city's labyrinthine alleys giving way to a neat grid of broad avenues and boulevards. Guéliz is the heart of the New Town and home to many of its best

*Hand-shaped door knocker*

*City wall*

restaurants and shops; south of here, the leafy Hivernage district houses a number of the city's top hotels, notably La Mamounia.

Marking the division between the Medina and the Ville Nouvelle is the Koutoubia Mosque, built by the Almohad Dynasty (1147–1248). The soaring minaret, with its distinctive brass pinnacle, is a useful orientation point day and night (when it is illuminated). From here it is a pleasant 30-minute walk along the broad, leafy Avenue Mohammed V to the heart of Guéliz, Place Abdel Moumen Ben Ali. Buses ply the route or it's around 25DH by taxi.

### Routes out of the city

Beyond Guéliz routes head west and north, with a motorway stretching 600km (360 miles) to Tangier, at Morocco's northernmost tip. South of Marrakech roads lead to the two great passes through the High Atlas Mountains: via the Tizi-n-Tichka pass to Ouarzazate, and over the Tizi-n-Test to Taroudant, gateways to Morocco's deep south and the Sahara. If these are closed after heavy snowfall, the only passage south is via the less interesting Imi-n-Tanoute to Agadir. There is no railway south of Marrakech.

### TOURISM BOOM

Tourism in Marrakech is nothing new. Writing in as far back as 1938, George Orwell was already complaining that the city had become 'utterly debauched by the tourist racket'. The city has long had its devotees, from Winston Churchill to Yves Saint Laurent to the Rolling Stones. But it was a programme of sustained investment and public initiatives – from creating parks and gardens to the construction of the Palais des Congrès conference venue and the Théâtre Royal – that really saw the city take off. The liberalisation of property laws to encourage foreign buyers also saw a flood of expats arriving to set up home in the city, and direct budget flights from many places in Europe also helped massively, transforming the city from a (reasonably) well-kept secret into one of Africa's most popular tourist destinations. Fresh initiatives continue with the construction of a third airport terminal and the spectacular renovation of La Mamounia, Morocco's most famous hotel.

### ROOMS TO RENT

Hotel capacity in the city has increased massively since the mid-noughties, with large chain hotels going up in the Hivernage area and the Palmeraie, and countless medina riads (traditional courtyard houses) being bought and restored by Western expats. The city has absorbed these additions surprisingly well. The large hotels are set well apart, in their own leafy enclave, and the riads are unobtrusive, their idyllic microworlds contained behind high walls that

*Shoppers in one of the souks*

are indistinguishable from surrounding buildings.

There is an ongoing debate about the pros and cons of gentrifying the medina, but by and large it is seen as preferable to the steady dereliction of the old town that had begun to set in, as established *Marrakshi* families moved to more spacious properties in the New Town, and the older properties were neglected.

## WORK, WORK, WORK

Marrakech is the natural magnet for the High Atlas tribes who have migrated to the city in an attempt to make a better life. Small surprise then that the city has a reputation for hard work among other Moroccans; despite Marrakech's festival atmosphere, daily life here is considered tough, and traditionally people rise early and work late. There are some sobering statistics behind the glossy image of a country characterised by chic riads and designer cafés: some 23 percent of Moroccans (including 43 percent of women) are illiterate, and unemployment rates currently hover around the 18 percent mark. Unlike Casablanca and Rabat, the city has few pretentions to sophistication and a very small middle class.

## ROYAL CONNECTIONS

In spite (or because) of its large working-class population, Marrakech has long been a favourite getaway of the Moroccan royal family. The late King Hassan II (1929–99) spent a lot of time here (especially on the golf courses) and began the massive investment in the city that his son Mohammed VI has consolidated. The Alaouite Dynasty, to which they belong, originated in the south of Morocco in the Tafilalt (a remote though well-populated valley below the Atlas), and the family has tended to favour the 'capital of the south' over the more cultured cities of the north.

The extensive royal palace takes up a substantial chunk of the southern

## A feudal land

Every year the king's sovereignty is underlined in the Act of Allegiance, a centuries-old ceremony in which tribal chiefs, religious leaders and high-ranking officials pledge their loyalty and obedience by bowing low and kissing the sovereign's hand. In many other monarchies, this might seem like a cherished tradition redolent of a bygone age, but in Morocco it is an accurate reflection of the country's feudal nature. In spite of Mohammed VI's modernising moves since acceding to the throne, he remains all-powerful. Although there are multi-party elections, the king personally appoints the prime minister, senior ministers and judges, is head of the armed forces, and, as 'Commander of the Faithful', is spiritual leader too.

*Cyber Parc, Guéliz*

*Majorelle Garden*

half of the medina (although Moham-med VI has built a new palace on Rue Sidi Mimoun), meaning that pedestrians have to make long detours. Similarly, much of the medina's northern half is taken up by the old Dar el Bacha, the for-

## DON'T LEAVE MARRAKECH WITHOUT...

**Getting lost in the souks.** Dive into the souks and follow your instincts for a taste of Marrakech at its labyrinthine best. See page 34.

**Drinking a mint tea.** Sweet, but with a hint of tantalising astringency, mint tea is the classic Moroccan beverage and some-thing of a social ritual all of its own. The terrace at the Café des Epices is a per-fect place to enjoy a pot of the national brew while taking in the bustling life of the souks. See page 39.

**Sampling a traditional tajine.** Served siz-zling hot straight from the oven, the clas-sic tajine offers the quintessential taste of Morocco. Recipes range from tongue-tingling citrus- and olive-flavoured recipes to comforting slow-cooked stews suffused with the aroma of dried fruits and almonds. See page 15.

**Visiting a hammam.** Unwind, Moroc-can style, with a visit to a local hammam, washing the city grime out of your pores before submitting to an enthusiastic *gommage* by the resident masseur. See page 24.

**Exploring the Jemma el Fna.** Spend an evening on one of the world's greatest public spaces, starting with an evening meal at one of the square's smoke-swathed cafés and then weaving through the crowds to enjoy the myriad musicians,

snake-charmers, story-tellers and other performers on display. See page 32.

**Experiencing the marvel of old Mar-rakech.** Make time to explore the monu-ments and palaces of old Marrakech, from the crumbling grandeur of the El Badi Pal-ace to the hidden cemetery of the magical Saadian Tombs. See page 49.

**Staying in a riad.** Offering an opulent taste of medina life, a stay in one of the city's lux-urious old-style Moroccan courtyard man-sions can't be beaten, either for traditional ambience or contemporary hedonism. See page 100.

**Exploring Guéliz.** It's a far cry from the picture-postcard image of traditional Mar-rakech, but to understand what makes the contemporary city tick, spend some time in Guéliz, the vibrant heart of Marrakech's New Town (Ville Nouvelle). Spend an after-noon browsing the district's chic bou-tiques, then head off to one of the area's many cosmopolitan bars and restaurants for a sight of the city's bright young things at play. See page 54.

**Driving the road to Ait-Benhaddou.** One of Morocco's classic road-trips, from Mar-rakech up into the mountains of the High Atlas, past remote Berber villages and over the wild Tizi-n-Tichka pass before descending to the picturesque mudbrick village of Ait-Benhaddou. See page 86.

*Aït-Benhaddou village*

mer palace of Thami El Glaoui (aka the Pasha of Marrakech), a tribal chief who colluded with the French in the first half of the 20th century.

### The cult of king

Many buildings open to the public – offices, shops, restaurants, cafés – have a portrait of Mohammed VI on their walls. Although no longer obligatory, as it was under the autocratic Hassan II, this practice reflects the huge reverence paid to the king as both head of state and 'Commander of the Faithful'. The latter title derives from the Alaouites' descent from the Prophet Mohammed and is the king's best defence against Islamic radicalism.

## RELIGION

For an Islamic country, Morocco is outwardly very tolerant, and Marrakech particularly so. Alcohol is permitted, women dress as they please, government censorship appears to be relatively light, and there is even an Ibiza-style nightclub (Pasha) on the city's southern outskirts. Despite much grinding poverty and the meagre benefits of trickle-down economics, it is hard to imagine hardline Islamicism taking root in easy-going Marrakech. That said, in 2011 the city was targeted by bombers in a deadly attack that left 17 people – most of them tourists – dead. Exactly who perpetrated the attack and why remains unclear.

But for the visitor to underestimate the importance of religion in the city would be a mistake. Mohammed VI's liberalisation of traditionally orientated family laws, derived from sharia, was fiercely resisted by large sections of society. The mosques, too, are busy, even in the city centre. As the muezzin's call to sunset prayer reverberates around the Jemaa el Fna, the musicians and entertainers fall silent, and a surprising number of people drift off into the mosques to pray.

## A GARDEN CITY

Despite being situated on a dry and stony plain, with little rainfall even in winter, Marrakech is an extraordinarily green city. Underground springs gave life to the Palmeraie (the huge oasis of date palms off the Casablanca road) many centuries ago, and successive dynasties mastered the art of irrigation, tapping into the water table to create orchards, olive groves and palace gardens.

In his travelogue *Escape with Me!* (1939), the British writer Osbert Sitwell called Marrakech the 'ideal African city of water-lawns, cool, pillared palaces and orange groves'. Today, visiting gardeners will find lots to interest them in the Majorelle Garden, El Bahia Palace, La Mamounia Hotel and the Cyber Parc, from towering cacti to poinsettia trees – striking full-grown versions of the ubiquitous Christmas pot plants.

*Pouring tea in a carpet shop*

*Traditional restaurant*

## TOP TIPS FOR EXPLORING MARRAKECH

**Beat the crowds.** Many of Marrakech's leading attractions get regularly swamped with tour groups. Visiting either at the beginning or end of the day is a good idea.

**Follow the signs.** If you get lost in the medina, look out for the overhead signs for the Jemaa el Fna or other major landmarks at road junctions – a great way of avoiding falling into the clutches of faux-guides, carpet-sellers or other hustlers looking to make a quick buck out of your temporary disorientation.

**Have fun bartering.** Bartering is a social interaction, not a competitive sport. Keeping a smile on your face and a friendly attitude works better than becoming aggressive. If you think you're being ripped off, then just walk away.

**Never name a price for something you don't intend to buy.** Never start bartering and name a price for an item unless you're prepared to buy it at that price. Failure to do so is considered the height of bad manners at the very least.

**Don't be intimated.** Make no mistake, the pressure to buy in Marrakech can sometimes be intense, especially if you get caught in a carpet shop. Don't be intimidated though. However many rugs may have been unfurled for your inspection, and however many cups of mint tea you've consumed, if you don't want to buy anything, just stand up and walk away.

**Carry cash.** There are no ATMs in the Marrakech souks, and plastic is usually accepted only for major purchases. If you intend to do a bit of shopping, make sure you have sufficient cash before diving in.

**Make a reservation.** Despite the incredible number of hotels and restaurants in Marrakech, the very best places can get booked up weeks, sometimes months, in advance. If you've got your heart set on staying or eating in a particular place, book as soon as you possibly can.

**Learn a little Arabic.** Arabic is a difficult language – Moroccan Arabic even more so – but it is polite to try mastering at least the most common greetings and phrases. A smattering of French may also help.

**Take photographs responsibly.** Don't go shoving your camera or phone into people's faces willy-nilly assuming they'll be happy to have their photos taken – women especially. Always ask permission before taking people's photographs, and be aware that some *Marrakshis*, such as the water-sellers on the Jemaa el Fna, will expect payment in return for that perfect snap.

**Agree a price beforehand.** Never get into a taxi or a *calèche* without agreeing a price beforehand and don't take a tour without confirming the price with your guide.

**Watch your back.** Many of Morocco's medinas and kasbahs are increasingly plagued by kamikaze motorcyclists who go shooting through the crowds at reckless speed – keep to the side of the road and try to stay alert to the hazards of approaching traffic both in front and behind.

*Cooking in tajines*

# FOOD AND DRINK

*There are restaurants absolutely everywhere in Marrakech, serving up a huge range of international and local fare, as well as dozens of top-notch places showcasing the very best of Morocco's celebrated cuisine.*

Gone are the days when dining out in Marrakech was a choice between French classics in an old-fashioned restaurant in Guéliz or a *couscous royale* in a cavernous and half-empty palais in the medina. Now you can also enjoy Italian, Spanish, Japanese, Indian, Thai and modern European food in stylish settings. Top chefs have been drawn to the city, such as Michelin-starred Fabrice Vulin, of Dar Ennasim fame (see page 118).

## MOROCCAN CUISINE

International interest in Moroccan cuisine has taken it out of the home and into some very sophisticated restaurant kitchens, where it is often fused with other (particularly French) influences to create exciting new tastes. Flavoursome meat, fruit and vegetables, plus top-quality fish rushed in at the crack of dawn from Essaouira and Agadir, also make Marrakech an interesting place for cooks and gourmets. Indeed, several enterprising riads and hotels specialise in providing Moroccan cookery lessons in addition to the usual programme of excursions and activities. Among the best regarded is at La Maison Arabe (see page 112), near Bab Doukkala.

## STREET FOOD

At the other end of the scale, the Moroccan pleasure in food is reflected in the array of snacks sold from makeshift stands on street corners or hawked by a vast army of vendors. Cauldrons of

---

### Ramadan specialities

Ramadan may be the month of fasting, but the daily breaking of the fast at sundown is eagerly anticipated and several special dishes are served during this time. The most important is *harira*, a meaty soup (lamb or chicken) with chickpeas and sometimes egg, flavoured with chopped coriander and a squeeze of lemon juice. Almost everyone ends their fast with a bowl, sometimes accompanied by dates and milk, followed by *shebakkia*, knots of deep-fried pastry dipped in honey or syrup and sprinkled with sesame seeds. If you want to try *harira* outside Ramadan, several of the food-stalls on the Jemaa el Fna serve it.

---

*Charcoal-grilled lamb*

snails in a cumin-flavoured liquor (try the Jemaa el Fna or Place des Epices), pans of freshly made tortilla, trays of soft sugared doughnuts *(sfenj)*, newspaper cones of freshly roasted nuts or hand-made potato crisps (quite possibly fried in a sawn-off oil drum) are just a few of the tasty temptations found on a stroll through the medina.

Everything is beautifully displayed, from the pyramids of olives and coloured spices in the markets to skewers of lamb fresh off the grill and fanned out on palm leaves.

## STAPLE DISHES

In restaurants, the once-ubiquitous couscous has lost out to the more versatile tajine in the popularity stakes, but it remains a firm favourite in Moroccan homes, especially at lunchtime on Friday, when it is traditionally served after prayers at the Friday Mosque.

### Couscous and tajines

Couscous is usually topped with a stew of chicken or lamb, chickpeas, courgettes, turnips, tomatoes and carrots, and accompanied by a glass of *laban* (a sour-tasting cultured milk).

Tajines – tasty stews served in distinctive pots with conical lids – come in many delicious guises, and are where many of the subtleties and surprises of Moroccan cuisine are found. They frequently pair sweet and savoury, or savoury and sour, with knockout results.

Typical combinations are beef with quinces, lamb with dates and apricots, or beef with almonds and whole hard-boiled eggs. One of the most common tajines is chicken with preserved lemons and olives *(djej maqalli)*.

Meat is always cooked slowly in large slabs or on the bone and presented in a large flat dish placed in the centre of the table, to which everyone tucks in. Dishes of olives, sliced and salted cucumber, roasted aubergine mashed with garlic, lemon and olive oil, mixed pickles and other salads are served on the side, along with warm flatbread.

### Pastilla

More unusual, as it is time-consuming and difficult to make, is *pastilla*, a dish of layered *warkha* pastry interleaved with pounded pigeon breast (although other ingredients, usually chicken, are sometimes substituted), mixed with saffron, egg, spices and almonds, and finished with a dusting of icing sugar. Traditionally a festive dish, good *pastilla* can be ordered in the more exclusive restaurants; an average restaurant is unlikely to do it well.

### Sweets

At home, meals normally end with fruit followed by mint tea and home-made sweets. These tend to be made of filo pastry, with honey, dates, figs, almonds or pistachios, although chocolate is also popular. 'Gazelles' horns' (crescents of sweet pastry with an almond and sem-

*Chicken pastilla*

olina filling) are typical. Plain sweetened yoghurt, often home-made, or ricotta mixed with honey and sesame are other great ways to finish a meal. Shop-bought European-style pastries, with confectioner's custard and fancy glazes, are often bought for special occasions.

### The Moroccan menu

*The following is a selection of some of the most popular Moroccan dishes.*

*bessara:* Broad (fava) beans mashed with paprika, cumin, oil, garlic and olive oil.

*briouats:* Delicious deep-fried envelopes of *warkha* (filo) pastry filled with minced lamb and herbs, cheese or egg.

*brochettes:* Lamb, chicken, beef or liver grilled on skewers over charcoal. Brochette stands are everywhere, and on major roads, grill restaurants, serving brochettes, *merguez*, *kefta* and lamb cutlets, cluster around junctions.

*couscous:* Semolina grains. Morocco's national dish is a meat, vegetable and chickpea stew on a steaming bed of couscous. Fish and vegetable couscous is also found. Two popular kinds of couscous include one with seven vegetables and another with caramelised onions, raisins and chickpeas.

*douara:* Tasty casserole of marinated lamb's tripe, liver and heart, popular after Aid el Kebir festival, when each family buys and slaughters a lamb.

*harira:* A Moroccan soup of lamb, lentils, chickpeas, noodles, egg and more, spiced with cinnamon, ginger, cayenne, turmeric and coriander.

*harissa:* A spicy red-pepper paste often served with grilled meats.

*hergma:* Calves' feet. A few stalls on the Jemaa el Fna specialise in this delicacy.

*hout/samek:* The Arabic words for fish (*tagine bel hout*, for example, is a fish tajine), but on menus fish is usually listed by type in French: *thon* (tuna), *loup de mer* (sea bass), *rouget* (red mullet), *dorade* (sea bream), *merlan* (whiting), *homard* (lobster), and *crevettes* (prawns). A spicy chermoula marinade is sometimes used to improve the taste of large white fish.

*kefta:* Meatballs flavoured with coriander and cumin, and often served with a fried egg and *harissa* on the side. A widely available great-tasting standby.

*khobz:* Bread. Mainly comes in two kinds: French or small, flat wholemeal loaves.

*laban:* A sour-tasting cultured milk that is traditionally served with couscous.

*mechoui:* A dish of spit-roasted lamb for special occasions. Often served at oriental entertainments.

*merguez:* Spicy lamb or beef sausages, sometimes served with fried eggs or as part of a mixed grill, with a dollop of *harissa*.

*pastilla:* An intricate pie (traditionally filled with pigeon, though chicken of fish are sometimes substituted) baked in layered *warkha* pastry and topped with a dusting of sugar.

*samek: See hout.*

*tajine:* The name for both the cooking vessel and the recipe, the latter being a tasty stew of meat and vegetables. Var-

*Mint tea*                    *Orange-juice carts*

iations include chicken with lemon and olives, beef with prunes and almonds, lamb with dates and apricots.

## DRINKS

### Tea

Tea is as much an institution amongst Moroccans as it is for the Japanese or British. Brewed in distinctive silver-coloured teapots with fresh mint and sugar, it is poured into delicate glasses, often from a height to cool and aerate the hot liquid. Mint tea (thé à la menthe) is refreshing at any time of day, but is especially good as a digestive.

### Juice

The orange-juice sellers on the Jemaa el Fna are as much a part of the scene as the acrobats and snake charmers. Their drinks cost as little as 4DH – a quarter of what the same thing will cost in any nearby café. Fresh apple, pear, banana, almond and even avocado juices (the last two sweetened and liquidised with milk) are all available in season. Sugar is often added automatically, so if you don't want it, be sure to say so, though you might find a small amount is nicer than none.

### Alcoholic drinks

Alcohol is served in the more expensive restaurants and café-bars, hotels and nightclubs. Until fairly recently, it was impossible to buy alcohol in the medina, but laws were relaxed when the riad phenomenon took hold, and you will now find late-night drinking haunts such as Kosybar (see page 48), overlooking Place des Ferblantiers in the heart of the old town. The national brews are Flag, Stork and Casablanca, lager-type bottled beers that sell for 30–60DH depending on the venue.

Moroccan wine has come a long way in recent years. It is mainly produced around Meknes and Casablanca. Good reds include Côteaux de l'Atlas, Beni M'Tir Larroque Cabernet Sauvignon and Merlot blend, and Médaillon Cabernet from the Domaine des Ouled Thaleb vineyard. Whites to try include Beauvallon Chardonnay from the Beni M'Tir vineyard and the Médaillon Cabernet Blanc. A recommended place to sample Moroccan wines is Kosybar. The owner's father is the proprietor of the award-winning Les Celliers de Meknes vineyard, and he has a good selection of both their own and other wines.

## Food and Drink Prices

Throughout this guide, we have used the following price ranges to denote the approximate cost of a three-course meal for one, excluding drinks:

€€€€ = over 500DH
€€€ = 250–500DH
€€ = 100–250DH
€ = under 100DH

*Souk shopping*

# SHOPPING

*The extensive souks of Marrakech are very much a highlight of a visit to Morocco. But the city also has a sprinkling of chic boutiques and an out-of-town shopping quarter showcasing the best of modern Moroccan design.*

Marrakech has lived by trade for centuries. Built on the crossroads of global caravan routes, and the chief trading centre for the tribes of the High Atlas, it has long been a place where raw materials have been bought and sold and then turned into luxury goods that can also be traded.

The best times to shop are the morning, when business is brisk and efficient, and early evening when *Marrakshis* pour into the souks not just to buy but to browse and soak up the atmosphere: the gorgeous colours, the twinkling lights, the smell of mint and spices.

Traditionally in Morocco, the men in the family do the shopping, perhaps to shield their wives from the cut and thrust of the marketplace, perhaps to control the purse strings. While this is no longer so true, you will still see more men than women in the souks.

## WHERE TO SHOP

### The souks

Like other ancient Islamic cities, Marrakech has an extensive network of souks, with each area of the souk devoted to a particular craft or trade. Stretching north of the Jemaa el Fna, the souks cover an area of about 4 sq km (1.5 sq miles), a vast labyrinth, partially roofed with makeshift mats or boards, which can quickly disorientate first-time visitors. Route 2 (see page 34) picks out the main areas.

For visitors, the most interesting sections of the souk remain the Souk des Babouches (slippers); Souk Cherratine (leather); the Kissarias (a series of small shopping arcades, mainly selling textiles); Souk Haddadine (the metalworkers souk, hung with a magical array of lanterns); Souk des Teinturiers (draped with colourful dyed fabrics); and Place des Epices, surrounded by a string of traditional herbalists, selling obscure medicines and other natural potions, and with women stallholders in the middle selling baskets, bags and hats (straw in summer and colourful rough woollen caps in winter). The main road through the souks, the Souk Attarine, is also interesting, if a lot more upmarket, with smart shops selling heirloom-quality traditional arts and crafts.

Other interesting souks include the attractive Place des Ferblantiers (see

*Slippers, Souk des Babouches*

page 47), for lanterns and brass-work in all shapes and sizes. Close by is the Grande Bijouterie, a slender alleyway of tiny shops crammed with amazingly ornate gold jewellery (see page 47). In addition, the Mouassine Quarter, west of the Mouassine Mosque, has a number of small boutiques selling more unusual items such as clothes, gifts and tableware, often based on traditional crafts but given a contemporary twist.

Shops in the souks follow no set hours, but most open roughly Saturday to Thursday from 10am to 9pm (some, but by no means all, close for a long lunch from around 1pm) and Friday from 10am to noon. Shops in Guéliz follow Western opening hours, usually around Monday to Saturday from 10am to 7.30pm, possibly with an hour off for lunch.

### New Town

In the Ville Nouvelle (New Town), several of the side streets off Avenue Mohammed V in Guéliz are worth exploring, particularly Rue de la Liberté, where you'll find a number of shops offering more refined versions of traditional handicrafts.

### Sidi Ghanem Industrial Zone

If you are seriously interested in contemporary Moroccan design, or are looking to export larger traditional pieces such as well-made *zellige* (mosaic-tiled) table-tops, wrought-iron garden furniture or tiles, pay a visit to the purpose-built Sidi Ghanem Industrial Zone, off Route de Safi (northwest exit from the city). The trip should cost around 300-400DH return by taxi, including waiting time.

Among the showrooms are Akkal (no. 322) for stunning ceramics and textiles; Via Notti (next door to Akkal) and Angie (no. 391), both of which sell fine linens and other fabrics; Amira Bougies (no. 277), offering handmade candles; and Atelier Nihal (no. 366), which sells stylish cushions, throws and other soft furnishings. Slightly further out along the same road, Tala-manzou (932 Résidence al Massar, Route de Safi, on the right-hand side of the Safi road as you leave town) offers some interesting new slants on traditional Moroccan carpets.

### WHAT TO BUY

### Carpets and blankets

Carpets are sold in all quarters of the souks, but especially in Souk des Tapis, off Place des Epices. Chichaoua and Sidi Moktar, on the way to Essaouira, are also considered good places to buy carpets.

You will find tufted carpets and *kilims* (flat-weave rugs), often in shades of red and yellow, with geometric patterns and symbols such as lozenges, crosses and stylised eyes to deflect *djinn* (supernatural spirits). Carpets sold in markets are both machine- and hand-made; it is better to visit one of

*Souk Haddadine sells metalwork*

the more reputable carpet shops, such as Bazaar du Sud in Souk des Tapis, off Place des Epices, if you want one of the latter. Examine the back of the carpet: a genuine handwoven rug will be far from perfectly finished.

### Ceramics

Several of the more upmarket shops in Guéliz (L'Orientaliste, at 11 and 15 Rue de la Liberté, and La Porte d'Orient, 6 Boulevard el Mansour Eddahbi, for example) have stunning (and expensive) traditional and/or antique tableware for sale, usually from Fez and Meknes.

For cheaper versions, however, examine the items displayed along the exit roads from town. Like carpets, the massive serving plates and vases can be quite hard to resist, but note that they tend to chip quite easily. The glazed tajine pots are for serving tajines rather than for cooking them, though the earthenware ones can be used over charcoal and often come with a stand to hold the hot coals. Beware patio pots that will not withstand frost.

You may also find inexpensive earthenware cups decorated with a black resin derived from the thuya tree (see page 21). The resin's distinctive medicinal smell has the advantage of repelling insects.

### Edibles

A selection of Moroccan sweets makes a good gift to take home. There are plenty of shops where you can buy them, but check out the ones in Rue de la Liberté in Guéliz or visit Amandine (see page 57).

Other edibles worth buying are olives, of which there are many varieties and almost as many different ways of preparing them, and jars of preserved lemons (a staple of Moroccan cuisine). Investigate the Marché Central, off Avenue Mohammed V (behind Plaza Marrakech) in Guéliz, for these.

### Beauty products

Argan oil is widely sold, both in Marrakech and in Essaouira, where it is produced from the fruit of argan trees, a thorny low-growing tree that is found only in this region. The oil is used in cooking but is also valued for its restorative properties and is used in shine-inducing hair shampoos, conditioners and treatments plus soaps, face creams and other beauty potions and lotions.

### Leatherware

Moroccan leather is of very good quality. For the most dazzling displays of *babouches*, the soft slippers with the turned-down heels, visit the Souk des Babouches (see page 36) in the northern half of the medina. The slippers range from the very glamorous — sequin-encrusted, embroidered with silver thread, and in many gorgeous colours — to utilitarian brown, red or yellow varieties for men. White *babouches* are traditionally worn to the Friday Mosque.

*Spices for sale*                    *Carpets at Place des Epices*

Jackets, handbags, briefcases, lampshades and pouffes are found everywhere. In Guéliz, Place Vendôme (141 Avenue Mohammed V, on the corner of Rue de la Liberté) has a good selection of quality items.

### Metalware

This is a speciality of Marrakech. Items range from massive brass door-knockers and hinges to wrought-iron furniture and grilles, and from the curvy silver-coloured teapots (which make ideal souvenirs) to highly patterned copper or brass trays and vases that cover every inch of many an Aladdin's cave. The quality varies tremendously but, once you've shopped around a little bit, it is not difficult to get a sense of this. For decorative lanterns seek out Souk Haddadine (see page 37) or Place des Ferblantiers (see page 47).

For quality decorative items try shops such as L'Orientaliste and La Porte d'Orient (see page 20), which also sell some amazing examples of antique Berber jewellery: massive brooches and *kuhl-kahl* (anklets), necklaces, earrings and rings.

### Woodwork

Sections of old doors, *mashrabiyyah* screens and old painted wooden chests and tables have become much sought-after in recent years. Shops such as La Porte d'Orient (see page 20) have some very fine examples. However, you will also find such items in the souks,

though be aware that 'antique' pieces may simply be expertly distressed.

Much cheaper are the many different items (including chess sets and furniture) made from the distinctively marked thuya wood of the Essaouira region. Be aware, however, that the indigenous tree from which this comes is endangered – it's best to buy any such products from environmentally conscious cooperatives.

## The art of haggling

Haggling is an intrinsic part of Moroccan culture, which visitors to Morocco either embrace and enjoy, or loathe to such a degree that they avoid shopping altogether.

There are no hard-and-fast rules to this mind-game, other than never start haggling for something you have no intention of buying (time-wasters are not tolerated kindly) and start your negotiations well below the asking price (a third is often suggested).

If you don't enjoy haggling, you could seek out the fixed-price government-run shop Ensemble Artisanal, opposite the Cyber Parc on Avenue Mohammed V (see page 54). Most shops in Guéliz also display price tags, but even here, don't be afraid to make the shopkeeper an offer (although not substantially below the asking price). The only thing one doesn't haggle for, even in markets, is food.

*Camel riding in Essaouira*

# ACTIVITIES

*The beautiful countryside around Marrakech provides plenty of scope for outdoor activities ranging from horse-riding to mountain trekking, while the wild coastline at nearby Essaouira offers world-class watersports in abundance.*

Marrakech is the ideal sybarite's city – souks, spas, riads, restaurants and year-round fine weather positively encourage endless idling and lounging, although there are plenty of more energetic activities out there if you feel the urge to pick yourself up off the poolside terrace and get moving again.

## PERFORMING ARTS

The city has few cultural venues in the European sense, but there is more going on than is at first apparent. For listings of latest events visit www.madein-marrakech.com.

The most active venues are the Théâtre Royal, at 40 Boulevard Mohammed VI in Guéliz, which stages concerts and exhibitions, and the Institut Français (see page 120) on the Route de Targa, which organises concerts, films and exhibitions.

Other events – exhibitions, concerts, jazz evenings – are held in Dar Cherifa (see page 41) and also in café-restaurants such as the Café du Livre (see page 57) and and Le Grand Café de la Poste (see page 116).

For more information on cultural events in the city, see page 120.

## HIKING AND BIKING

Marrakech is the natural springboard for treks in the Atlas, particularly the Toubkal National Park (see page 80). Various treks, ranging from one-day hikes in the Atlas foothills to a three-day ascent of Mount Toubkal can easily be arranged in Marrakech.

Morocco Adventure Tours (www.moroccoadventuretours.com) offers a wide range of hiking, canyoning and quad biking trips, as well as white-water rafting. Bespoke hiking tours can be set up through Mountain Voyage Morocco (5 Avenue Mohammed V, Guéliz; http://agents.mountain-voyage.com). Alternatively, head up to Imlil and make arrangements independently on the spot. The cost of hiring a mountain guide, who can organise food, mules and equipment if necessary, and staying in mountain lodges *(gîtes)* is set and published by the tourist board. The best time for hiking is late spring through to early autumn.

## GOLF

There are three good courses in Marrakech – each of them beautifully situ-

*Hiking in Morocco's deep south*

*Paragliding on the coast*

ated. Expect to pay about 600DH for 18 holes, plus 350DH green fees.

The state-of-the-art Al Maaden Golf Resort (Sidi Youssef Ben Ali; www.almaaden.com) opened in 2010 to a design by Kyle Phillips, with unusual water features designed to evoke the atmosphere of a Moroccan garden.

The 18-hole Amelkis course (Km 12, Route de Ouarzazate; tel: 0524-40 44 14) comprises an original 18-hole course, with a new nine-hole course added in 2009. Out in the Palmeraie Le Palmeraie Golf Club (www.palmeraiemarrakech.com), originally opened in 1992 to a Robert Trent Jones design, with a further nine holes added in 2008.

## HORSE RIDING

Marrakech's Palmeraie, Essaouira's beach and the foothills of the Atlas Mountains all offer wonderful horse riding. There are also specialist tour companies offering one- and two-week riding holidays, and several hotels in the Atlas can arrange riding for their guests. Expect to pay around 250DH per hour or 600DH for half a day.

Unicorn Trails (www.unicorntrails.com) is a UK-based outfit offering horse-riding tours in Marrakech and Essaouira.

The Atlas à Cheval ranch (932 Residence Al Massar, Route de Safi; tel: 0524-33 55 57), situated among olive groves about 26km (16 miles) from Mar-

rakech, offers good half- and full-day treks into the surrounding hills.

In Essaouria, the Ranch de Diabet (www.ranchdediabat.com) arranges horse and camel rides on the beach, into the surrounding countryside and to historic sites and marabouts.

## WATERSPORTS

Essaouira is internationally famous for its kite-surfing and windsurfing, and is also a popular surfing destination. The best conditions for surfing are at Moulay Bouzerktoun, 20km (12 miles) to the north, and Sidi Kaouki, 27km (17 miles) to the south.

In Essaouira itself, Club Mistral (www.club-mistral.com) and Magic Fun Afrika (www.magicfunafrika.com) both rent out windsurfing, kite-surfing and surfing equipment, as well as lessons. Just south of town in Sidi Kaouki, Windy Kaouki (www.windy-kaouki.com) can also help arrange watersports, as well as horse-riding trips.

## BALLOONING

Take to the skies for a memorable bird's-eye view of the Red City, surrounding palm groves and the snow-clad Atlas beyond. Flights are offered by Ciel d'Afrique (Imm. Ali, Appt.4, 2ème étage, Avenue Youssef Ben Tachfine; www.cieldafrique.info) and Marrakech by Air (184 Lala Haya, Marrakech; www.marrakechbyair.com).

*Relaxing in a hammam*

# HAMMAMS AND SPAS

*A soak and scrub in the hammam is an age-old ritual of Moroccan life, while numerous luxurious hammam-inspired retreats and spas are also springing up around the city to soothe the nerves of stressed-out visitors.*

The art of the hammam is an ancient and integral part of Moroccan life, where water, which is considered sacred, and cleanliness are essential elements of Islam. This is where people go to socialise, gossip, make connections, do business and even arrange marriages. There are one or more hammams in the medina of most towns and cities, some of them centuries old, some basic and others modern and luxurious.

Until fairly recently, only the wealthiest Moroccan homes had a properly equipped bathroom. Although people kept clean by washing with a jug and a bowl of water – ritual ablutions alone demand that Muslims wash five times a day before prayers – most of them went once a week to their local hammam for a thorough steam and *gommage* (exfoliation). Bathrooms are now far more widespread, but most Moroccans continue to go to their local hammam, partly for the deep-pore cleansing that domestic showers can't quite provide, but also for the social aspect of a visit.

For women, in particular, going to the hammam has always been a jolly social occasion, where, with children in tow, they can meet with their friends, gossip and joke, and might even take a sneaky look to check out which potential brides might be suitable for male members of their family.

For Moroccan men, the hammam tends to be a quieter place of rest and contemplation, where the week's mental stress is relieved while the resident masseur sets to work coaxing tensions out of knotted backs and shoulders.

## UPMARKET HAMMAMS

In recent years, the booming tourist industry has led to the creations of increasing numbers of upmarket spas and spa-style hammams (or hammam-style spas) – often places of decadent luxury, with deep blue pools, petal-strewn divans and state-of-the-art treatments a thousand miles from the traditional hammam. Upmarket hammams provide everything you will need and are fairly relaxed about nudity.

## LOCAL HAMMAMS

Neighbourhood hammams are often attached to the local bakery in order

*Candles and towels*

to share its furnace, while others can be found attached to mosques. Non-Muslims are generally more welcome in the former than in the latter. Marrakech's traditional hammams are of varying quality. Some of the more venerable places are handsome buildings with carved cedar ceilings, star-shaped skylights and other decorative features; others are Stygian places that seem more like breeding areas for germs than places of purification. In between these extremes, you'll find a host of functional modern establishments.

Local hammams have a changing area leading into a series of rooms of varying temperatures. You will be given a bucket for sluicing down with but are required to take your own soap, scrubbing mitt and towel, although locals are often happy to share soap (the traditional tar-like olive *savon noir*) and other equipment, if you don't have your own. The resident masseur (a massage is included in the price) will find you at some point during your visit to give you a good *gommage* and pummelling. If it all gets too much, just say *shwiya afak* (gently, please).

Note that it is usual to tip the various attendants a few dirhams.

### RECOMMENDED HAMMAMS

A selection of hammams in the Kasbah area (including one or two small establishments attached to riads) is given in route 5 (see page 51). Some other recommendations are given below.

### Hotel spas
Among the big hotels, The Palace Spa at Es Saadi (Avenue el Qadissia, Hivernage area; www.essaadi.com) and L'Hivernage Hotel and Spa (corner of Avenue Echouhada and Rue des Temples; www.hivernage-hotel.com) are particularly good, although most of the large hotels and the more exclusive riads now have spa facilities.

### Popular choices
Less luxurious but well-run, clean and functional is Hammam Ziani (14 Rue Riad Zitoun el Jdid; www.hammamziani.ma), near El Bahia Palace. For a good traditional local hammam, check out the 16th-century Hammam Bab Doukkala, next to the Doukkala Mosque on Rue Bab Doukkala. Like many smaller hammams, it is open to men in the morning and evening, and women in the afternoon.

In Guéliz one of the best-run spas, popular with well-heeled *Marrakshis*, is Les Secrets de Marrakech (62 Rue de la Liberté; tel: 0524-43 48 48), offering all sorts of tempting facials, massages and wraps.

Another good upmarket option is Les Bains de Marrakech (2 Derb Sedra, Bab Agnaou, Kasbah; www.lesbainsdemarrakech.com). This was one of the city's first luxury hammams, and is still considered one of the best.

*An 1836 engraving of Marrakech*

# HISTORY: KEY DATES

*Marrakech's fortunes have depended upon the tastes of the ruling dynasties. It was beautified by the Almoravids, Almohads and Saadians, ignored by the Merenids, but found favour again under Hassan II and Mohammed VI.*

### PRE-ISLAM

| | |
|---|---|
| **1100s BC** | Phoenician sailors establish a series of trading posts along Morocco's coast, including Karikon Telichos (modern-day Essaouira). |
| **146BC** | Carthage falls to Rome. Roman influence spreads west through North Africa. |
| **AD682** | First Arab raids on Morocco under the command of Oqba ibn Nafi. |

### ISLAM AND THE DYNASTIES

| | |
|---|---|
| **714** | Further Arab incursions into Morocco and Spain. Berbers embrace Islam and invade Spain under Arab leadership. |
| **788** | Idriss I, exiled from Baghdad, founds Morocco's first Arab dynasty. |
| **1060–1147** | The Almoravids, Berber warriors from Mauritania, sweep north, founding Marrakech as their capital. |
| **1147** | The Almohad dynasty, also Berber, rise out of the High Atlas and seize power, building the Koutoubia in Marrakech. |
| **1184** | The city's golden age under Yacoub el-Mansour sees a flourishing of arts and science. |
| **1269** | The Merenids conquer Marrakech, which subsequently goes into decline when the ruling Merenids chose Fez as their capital. |
| **1492** | Fall of Muslim Spain. |
| **1554–1669** | The Arab Saadian dynasty drives out the Christians. They base themselves in Marrakech, building the Saadian Tombs, El Badi Palace and the Ben Youssef Madrassa, and establish the *mellah*. |
| **1669** | Beginning of the present Alaouite dynasty. The Alaouite ruler Moulay Ismail moves the capital to Meknes, and Marrakech once again falls into decline for several centuries. |
| **1866** | El Bahia Palace is built. |

*French Minister at the Moroccan court (1909)*

## EUROPEAN ENCROACHMENT

| | |
|---|---|
| 1912 | The Treaty of Fez. Morocco is carved up between France and Spain. In Marrakech General Lyautey, the first Resident General, establishes the French-built New Town of Guéliz. |
| 1920s | Thami el Glaoui, Pasha of Marrakech, connives with the French, pacifying rebellious tribes in exchange for power and privileges. |
| 1953 | El Glaoui and 300 allies convene in Marrakech to draw up a proposal to replace the legitimate monarch (Sultan Mohammed Ben Youssef, later Mohammed V) with the elderly Ben Arafa. The true sultan and his family are exiled to Madagascar. |
| 1955 | Mohammed V is restored to the throne. |

## INDEPENDENCE

| | |
|---|---|
| 1956 | Independence granted. Mohammed V changes 'sultan' to 'king'. |
| 1961 | Accession of Hassan II. |
| 1963–77 | King Hassan survives the first of five different plots against him, the most serious of which are led by the army. |
| 1969 | Morocco, Marrakech in particular, becomes a regular stop on the hippie trail. |
| 1975 | The Green March: 350,000 unarmed Moroccans claim the Spanish (Western) Sahara for Morocco. |

## MODERN TIMES

| | |
|---|---|
| 1980s | Massive rural exodus towards the cities makes Marrakech Morocco's second-largest city. |
| 1999 | Hassan II dies. His son and successor, Mohammed VI, embarks on a programme of increased democratisation. |
| 2001 | Marrakech's International Film Festival is inaugurated. |
| 2002 | Mohammed VI marries. A son is born the following year. |
| 2009 | Fatima Zahar Mansouri becomes Marrakech's first female mayor. |
| 2010–11 | Peaceful protests are held across Morocco, demanding constitutional reform. Most Moroccans remain supportive of the king. |
| 2011 | Nail bomb detonated in Jemaa el-Fna in Marrakech. Some 17 people killed. No one claims responsibility. |
| 2013 | Mohammed VI appoints a new Islamist-led government. |

# BEST ROUTES

*Avenue Mohammed V*

# KOUTOUBIA MOSQUE AND JEMAA EL FNA

*Like different sides of the same coin – one sacred, one profane – the Koutoubia Mosque and the Jemaa el Fna together encapsulate Marrakech. They lie a short distance apart on either side of Place de Foucauld.*

**DISTANCE:** 1km (0.5 mile)
**TIME:** 2 hours
**START:** Koutoubia Mosque
**END:** Jemaa el Fna
**POINTS TO NOTE:** This route is best done late in the day, when the Koutoubia glows in the evening sun, locals come to stroll in the Koutoubia Gardens, and activity on the Jemaa el Fna, which is comparatively low-key during the day, starts to build up.

This is not so much a route linking two of the city's main sights as an immersion in the exhilarating atmosphere of Marrakech.

## KOUTOUBIA MOSQUE

The **Koutoubia Mosque** ❶ (Mosquée de la Koutoubia) is one of the icons of Marrakech. Its lovely ochre-coloured minaret rises like a beacon from **Place de Foucauld**, marking the point in the Old Town where the road to Guéliz in the Ville Nouvelle (see page 54) begins.

The interior is closed to non-Muslims, as it is a working mosque, but its exterior is worth a closer look.

### The Booksellers' Mosque

Begun by the Almohad sultan Abdel Moumin in 1158 and completed by Yacoub el Mansour, the Koutoubia, or Booksellers' Mosque, is thought to have been named after the scribes and Koran sellers who once plied their trade in the vicinity. It was not the Almohads' first attempt to construct a mosque on the site: excavations on the northern side of the complex have revealed bricked-up arches and the foundations of columns to support the roof of an earlier mosque, which may have been abandoned when it was discovered that it was not correctly aligned with Mecca.

### The minaret

The Koutoubia's **minaret** was the prototype for two other minarets in the Almohad Empire, the Tour Hassan in Rabat and the Giralda in Seville. It is nearly 70m (230ft) tall and follows the typical Almohad proportions of 1:5 (the height

*A sunlit wall*                    *The Koutoubia's minaret*

being five times the width). The exterior of the tower is decorated with stone tracery, each side displaying a different pattern. Originally, the unadorned stone would have been covered in plaster and decorated: bands of this decoration can still be seen near the top of the tower.

Behind the mosque, the **Koutoubia Gardens ②** (Jardins de la Koutoubia) are a popular place for an early evening stroll. Close to the road is the white **Koubba of Fatima Zohra ③**, the tomb of the daughter of a 17th-century holy man who was known for his compassion and named after the Prophet Mohammed's own daughter.

Across Avenue Mohammed V, the Islane Hotel's terrace restaurant offers a tempting view of the mosque and the animated evening scene. Unfortunately, it is a bit of a tourist trap, serving mediocre food. Instead, head east to the Jemaa el Fna to eat. En route you'll cross the spacious, tree-shaded **Place de Foucauld ④**, the main departure point for calèche (carriage) rides, although you will also find ranks outside the big hotels (for information on prices and routes, see page 64). The square also marks the beginning of Avenue Mohammed V, which runs from here up to Guéliz.

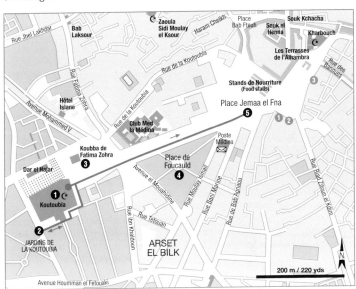

*Evening on the Jemaa el Fna*

### JEMAA EL FNA

The Koutoubia may be a favourite place for *Marrakshis* to congregate in the early evening, but it is a mere backwater in comparison with the heaving sea of humanity that congregrates on the **Jemaa el Fna ❺**.

## The Almohads

The Almohads, or al-Muwahhidun as they were originally called, conquered Marrakech in 1147. Bursting out of their tribal base in the N'fis Valley in the Atlas (see page 94), they descended upon the city, ousting the Almoravids, who had grown decadent after 90 years in power. From there they quickly spread north and east, and within a year they controlled the whole of Morocco. Eventually their empire stretched from Castile to Tripoli.

The greatest Almohad was Yacoub el Mansour ('the Victorious', 1184–99), whose reign saw a golden age in medicine, industry, architecture and the arts. However, as with the Almoravids, decline came within a century of seizing power. By 1230 the sultan was reduced to accepting 12,000 Christian cavalrymen from King Ferdinand of Castile and Leon in order to retake Marrakech from local dissidents. In 1248 the Almohads were defeated by the Merenids, another Berber tribe, who established their capital in Fez.

Variously translated as the place of the dead, place of destruction, or, most appropriately perhaps, the place of the apocalypse, the Jemaa el Fna is one of Africa's great squares. Despite the huge numbers of tourists in Marrakech, most of whom are drawn here at some point in the evening, it remains an intensely Moroccan place. The very heart of Marrakech, it defines the city's role as a marketplace and crossroads, where trans-Saharan trade caravans transporting salt, gold, sugar, spices and slaves once came to rest, the merchants seeking company and entertainment after weeks of hard travelling.

#### The entertainers

Today the camel trains are gone, but company and entertainment remain in abundance. Acrobats and storytellers draw the crowds, as do the fakirs – medicine-cum-holy men with cures for everything from impotence to possession by *djinn* (demons) plus charms to fend off the evil eye. Fortune-tellers are also plentiful, although you will be hard-pressed to find one who speaks English. You also can't fail to notice the *gerrab* (water-sellers) with their tasselled hats, studded leather girdles and necklaces of polished brass cups. A cup of water from a gerrab's goat-skin will cost a few dirhams, a photograph rather more.

Tourists tend to be targeted by women offering henna tattoos and snake-charmers. Usually belonging to the

*One of the many food stalls*                     *A snake-charmer*

Assioua brotherhood, a Sufi sect founded in the 15th century by the mystic healer Sidi ben Aissa, snake-charmers don't just perform for tourists. Both revered and feared for their powers, they have a steady business in ridding properties of poisonous snakes and scorpions.

You will always find at least one or two bands of *gnaoua* musicians. Distinguished by their cowrie-trimmed hats and waistcoats, these black musician-healers are believed to be descended from West African slaves brought to Morocco by the Saadians in the 16th century. Often their performances are fairly tame, but when the vibe and audience are right, their music will continue until dawn, the hypnotic rhythms of the *darbuka* beating a very African refrain.

### A ringside seat

Cooking up a storm in the centre of the square are rows of food stalls. This is the place to sample sizzling merguez sausages, brochettes, bowls of *harira* (a hearty soup), snails in a cumin-flavoured liquor, and, for the more adventurous, sliced sheep's head, tripe, calves' feet and much more. Trade is brisk, standards of hygiene reasonably well policed, and, providing you keep track of the prices, your bill will be low. Alternatively, there are several café-restaurants with terraces offering views over the mesmerising scene; recommendations for cafés are given in the Food and Drink box, see ❶, ❷ and ❸, while those for a more substantial meal are detailed in the listings (see page 110). Any of these is a good place to start or end an evening on the square.

## Food and Drink

There are numerous places to eat on the square, and the following is just a selection of cafés. For a more substantial meal, check out our restaurant listings (see page 110).

### ❶ LE GRAND BALCON DU CAFÉ GLACIER

Attracting a healthy mix of locals and tourists, with some of the best Jemaa el Fna views anywhere around the square, either from the verandah or (better) the huge upstairs terrace.

### ❷ CAFÉ CTM

This is the café-terrace (for drinks only) of the long-established budget hotel of the same name. It is quieter than the neighbouring Le Grand Balcon du Café Glacier, but it also offers good views of the spectacle below.

### ❸ CAFÉ DE FRANCE

A major Jemaa el Fna landmark, this is the biggest and most touristy of the numerous cafés lining the square. Seats are at a premium (particularly on the two upstairs terraces), and prices are on the high side, but for views of the square, this place really can't be beaten.

*A busy souk*

# THE SOUKS AND BEN YOUSSEF MADRASSA

*North of the Jemaa el Fna, the souks of Marrakech are among the finest in the Islamic world, a labyrinth piled high with traditional crafts stretching up to the landmark Ben Youssef Mosque and its exquisite nearby madrassa.*

**DISTANCE:** 1.5km (1 mile)
**TIME:** A half-day
**START:** Café de France, Jemaa el Fna
**END:** Jemaa el Fna
**POINTS TO NOTE:** This route is best suited to the morning, when the souks are in full swing and the monuments are open. The souks are considerably quieter, and therefore less atmospheric, in the afternoon, and although the cool of the early evening unleashes a fresh burst of commercial activity, the monuments close by around 6 or 7pm.

Marrakech's medina is divided into two halves, separated by the Jemaa el Fna. To the south are the main buildings of the Alaouite Dynasty (1631 to the present day), including several palaces, the *mellah* (old Jewish ghetto) and the Kasbah (see page 44). Spreading north of the square are the city's labyrinthine souks, the most dazzling in Morocco, plus several of the city's oldest monu-

ments including the superb 16th-century Ben Youssef Madrassa.

Fortunately, the days when anyone entering the souks would be mobbed by would-be guides pressing their services are now long since gone. If you would like to use a qualified guide to help you navigate the maze, hire one through your hotel. Unofficial guides gather early in the morning outside Club Med on Place de Foucauld – their rates are low, but unfortunately they're likely to be more interested in getting you into shops in which they receive commission rather than actually showing you the sights.

### Etiquette

When exploring the medina it's useful to follow a few simple rules. Always dress respectfully and ask before you take people's photographs. As a general rule, try to keep to the right (especially if you hear one of the souk's overloaded porters approaching, usually shouting *Balak! Balak!* as they go in order to clear a path through the crowds). And on no account start bar-

*Decorative plates*  *Aromatic spices*

gaining over an item unless you've a genuine interest in purchasing it.

## THE SOUKS

Begin at the **Café de France** ❶ on the eastern side of the Jemaa el Fna (see page 32). With your back to the café follow the alleyway immediately opposite, heading through the **Souk el Henna** ❷ (where henna, nuts, dried fruit and pulses are sold). This brings you to an arch of lacy stucco, half hidden among the surrounding buildings, which marks the start of Souk Semmarine.

### Souk Semmarine

Through here, **Souk Semmarine** ❸, the main artery of the souks, stretches north. This used to be the souk of the blacksmiths who dealt specifically with horses and donkeys, but is now a vivid corridor of consumerism. If you more or less keep to this, you won't get lost; if you wander at random, you almost certainly will, although this will bring its own pleasures and surprises.

Souk Semmarine is home to some of Marrakech's most upmarket souvenir shops selling genuine antiques, towers of myriad-coloured carpets, and bags and *babouches* (slippers) of the finest calf- and goatskin. Pressure to buy is far lighter than it used to be; some shopkeepers lay off the sales patter entirely, making browsing not only possible but positively pleasurable.

### The spice souks

After about 500m/yds, look out for a busy right turn (signposted) into **Place des Epices** ❹ (Place Rahba Kedima). The edge of the square is ringed with the tiny shops of the city's traditional *herboristes*, piled high with spices and traditional cosmetics and medicines, while ladies selling straw hats and baskets fill the centre of the square. The shops of the *herboristes* are worth a close look. Among the remedies, such as cloves to alleviate toothache and cardamom for poor circulation, are giant gourds, animal parts, ostrich eggs and feathers that are used in magic spells or as talismans. Foreign visitors are usually thought to be mainly interested in the various aphrodisiacs on sale. The most notorious, Spanish Fly (used by the Marquis de Sade in the 18th century), was banned in Morocco in the 1990s.

In addition to the mountains of different spices, look out for *savon beldi* (local soap), a black, tar-like soap made from olives; baskets of henna leaves (plus tubes of ready-made paste); and antimony (kohl) to darken eye rims. The last is used to protect as well as to beautify: children's eyes are sometimes rimmed with kohl to ward off evil spirits, especially after birth or circumcision.

Overlooking the square (on the left as you enter) is the terrace of **Café des Epices**, see ❶, ideal for taking in the scene. Off the northern side of the square is the former slave market. Slaves were

*Woollen hats for sale*

traded here until 1912, when the French closed down what little remained of the market.

### Souk el Kebir and Souk Cherratine

Retracing your steps to where you turned into Place des Epices, continue a few metres north to a fork. Either route from here will eventually take you to the Ben Youssef Mosque and Madrassa on Place Ben Youssef. Our route takes the right-hand route, **Souk el Kebir ❺**, which leads there more or less directly.

Continue north, where a tight maze of alleyways offers all sorts of diversions, from musical instruments to saddles. On the way you will pass the **Souk Cherratine ❻**, where leather from local tanneries is worked into pouffes, slippers and bags.

### Souk des Babouches, Kissaria and Souk Haddadine

As a more interesting, but potentially more disorientating, alternative, you could take the left-hand

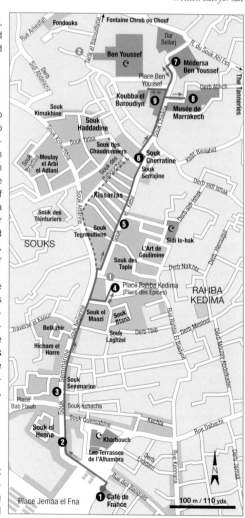

*Light and shade in the souks*

route from the fork just north of Place des Epices, heading via **Souk Attarine**.

Such is the popularity of the soft Moroccan slippers (*babouches*) with pointy toes and turned-down backs that **Souk des Babouches** (Souk Smata) has expanded into several neighbouring alleyways. Embroidered, bejewelled, and in countless gorgeous colours, the slippers can be hard to resist.

Running at right angles between Souk des Babouches and Souk el Kebir is the **Kissaria**, traditionally devoted to high-quality textiles and luxury goods, although nowadays replica football shirts take price of place. Look carefully, though, and you can still find top-quality kaftans and tailor-made garments.

North of Souk des Babouches, close to the Ben Youssef Mosque, is **Souk Haddadine** (Souk des Ferronniers), the metalworkers' souk. This is one of the most industrious in the medina, its presence announced by the noise of incessant hammering and pounding. Huge numbers of magical lanterns hang in virtually each shop, giving the entire souk a fairytale appearance.

### PLACE BEN YOUSSEF

This square is the location of three of Marrakech's main sights, the Ben Youssef Madrassa, the Koubba el Baroudiyn and the Museum of Marrakech. You can buy a good-value combined ticket for the museum and madrassa (or, alternatively, more expensive tickets for each one individually). Note that the **Ben Youssef Mosque** is closed to non-Muslims.

### BEN YOUSSEF MADRASSA

The largest of Morocco's historic *madrassas* (Koranic colleges), the **Ben Youssef Madrassa** ❼ (daily 9am– 6pm; charge) was begun in the 14th century by the Merenids, the dynasty most active in building *madrassas*. It was expanded by the Saadian sultan Abdallah el Ghallib, who wanted it to be the largest, most splendid of its kind in Morocco.

As is usual in Islamic architecture, the *madrassa*'s plain exterior walls give no hint of the staggering ornamentation inside, with every surface is covered in cedar and stucco carvings and *zellige* (mosaic tiling). In keeping with Islamic prescripts, representations of living creatures are notable by their absence. Instead, intricately executed floral and geometric motifs are repeated in mesmerising patterns, an effect intended to focus the mind on the infinite power and purpose of God.

#### Students' quarters

The two-storey complex centres on a marble courtyard with a rectangular pool. Around the edge of the courtyard on both levels are the students' quarters, 132 cells that would have been

*Ben Youssef Madrassa*

shared. The cells can be inspected (two have been furnished as they might have been at the time: one for a wealthy urban scholar, and one for a poor country student).

### Prayer hall

The prayer hall on the ground floor is divided with pillars of Carrara marble and has a magnificent cedar ceiling. It also has a carved stucco *mihrab* (niche indicating the direction of Mecca), depicting intertwining foliage, pine cones and Koranic verses, with traces of its original blue and red colouring.

## MUSEUM OF MARRAKECH

The **Museum of Marrakech** ❶ (Musée de Marrakech; daily 9am–6pm; charge) is housed in the Mnebhi Palace, the grand late 19th-century residence of Mehdi Mnebhi, a minister of Moulay Abdelaziz, the sultan whose profligate spending bankrupted the treasury and paved the way for European colonisation. The palace later became a property of Thami el Glaoui, the self-styled Pasha of Marrakech (see page 85) and then passed into state hands when Morocco gained independence in 1956. The building was restored and turned into a museum by the late Omar Benjelloun, a wealthy entrepreneur whose foundation also restored the Koubba el Baroudiyn.

### Moroccan arts and crafts

The museum provides a splendid setting for a collection of Moroccan arts and crafts, including jewellery, metalwork and carpets from the Anti-Atlas region, textiles from Fez and Tetouan, and ceramics from Fez and Safi.

The magnificent copper lantern over the central courtyard is 5m (16ft) in diameter and weighs 1,200kg (over one ton). You'll also find coins and calligraphy from across the Islamic world, as well as changing exhibitions by local and international artists. Items are dis-

---

## The tanneries

Heading east along Rue Souk el Fes (behind the Ben Youssef Madrassa) and then Rue Bab Debbarh brings you to the Marrakech tanneries. Along the way look out for the *fondouks* which line parts of the route; these old galleried inns, some several hundred years old, originally offered lodging for merchants and their animals.

The network of pits, in which the workers wade waist-deep, presents a scene that has barely changed in 1,000 years. Morocco has long been famous for its leather; at one time, whole European libraries were sent here to be morocco-bound. The overpowering smell emanates from the substance used to make the hides supple, a mix of pigeon droppings and animal urine; small bunches of mint are handed out to squeamish nose-holding visitors.

*Madrassa interior*                    *Museum of Marrakech*

played in the side rooms off the central courtyard, and in the old hammam, a domed complex studded with star-shaped skylights.

The courtyard café offers drinks and snacks, but for lunch try **Chez Abdelhay**, see ❷, behind Ben Youssef Mosque (follow the road round the mosque, passing the Koubba el Baroudiyn).

## KOUBBA EL BAROUDIYN

Just west of the Museum of Marrakech next door to the *Ben Youssef Mosque*, sits the unprepossessing **Koubba el Baroudiyn** ❾. The importance of this simple two-storey sandstone structure, the only Almoravid structure left in Marrakech (apart from a few sections of city walls), lies in its seminal role in the development of Hispano-Moorish architecture. The motifs and style that you see – the stepped battlements, the keyhole arches, the carvings inside the dome – have been repeated and elaborated through eight centuries of North African architecture.

You can't go inside the building, although there's a good view of it over the railings. Excavations have revealed the remains of a cistern, latrines and fountains, suggesting that the *koubba* formed the centre of an ablutions area for the nearby mosque, a far earlier incarnation of the 19th-century Ben Youssef Mosque that you see today.

A short distance up Rue Dour Saboun, just behind the Ben Youssef Mosque, is the 16th-century Chrob ou Chouf ('Drink and Look') Fountain. Like several other historic fountains, all in need of restoration, it is lavishly embellished with a finely carved cedar mantel.

Retrace your steps to the Jemaa el Fna – back along Souk el Kebir and Souk Semmarine is quickest; if you get lost, either ask a shopkeeper to point the way or look out for the helpful overhead signs posted all over the souks pointing in the direction of the Jemaa.

## Food and Drink

### ❶ CAFÉ DES EPICES

Place des Epices; tel: 0524-39 17 70, www.cafedesepices.net; 9am–8pm summer (6pm winter); €

Quaint, pocket-sized café overlooking Place des Epices, with ground-floor and first-floor terraces; the latter is more stylish with divan seating and views over the square. The selection of sandwiches, salads and light meals is perfect for a light lunch, although it can often get packed, so best to lunch early or late.

### ❷ CHEZ ABDELHAY

Behind the Ben Youssef Mosque; no tel.; €

A clean, friendly spot for a tasty mixed grill of brochettes, lamb cutlets and *kefta* with egg, accompanied by salad, olives, fresh bread and soft drinks. In sunny weather a handful of trestle tables are set up outside.

*Dar Cherifa's café*

# THE MOUASSINE QUARTER

*This route covers the area to the west of the main souks. It takes in the dyers' quarter, the beautifully restored Dar Cherifa, and the palace of the powerful Glaoui clan, who colluded with the French during the Protectorate.*

**DISTANCE:** 2km (1.25 miles)
**TIME:** A half-day
**START:** Jemaa el Fna
**END:** Koutoubia Mosque
**POINTS TO NOTE:** If time is limited you could pick up this route from Place Ben Youssef (see page 37), by heading west along Dyers' Souk to the Mouassine Mosque and Fountain.

The area to the northwest of the Jemaa el Fna is significantly different in character from the nearby souks, with wider streets, fewer crowds and a considerably calmer atmosphere. It's also home to several of the city's best riads and restaurants.

## STARTING OFF

Head north from the Jemaa el Fna (see page 32), keeping the food stalls on your right and continuing ahead until you reach **Place Bab Fteuh ❶**, a small triangular square busy with rather down-at-heel shops. Although the actual gate *(bab)* no longer exists, the spot retains the bustle of an entrance point.

Running off the northwest side of the square, **Souikat Laksour** leads up into the Mouassine Quarter, offering a sunnier and considerably quieter route through this part of town than the parallel Souk Semmarine (see page 35).

Souikat Laksour (and its continuation, Rue Mouassine) is also home to a number of interesting shops offering more unusual versions of the traditional crafts than you'll find in the main souks. These include Beldi (9–11 Souikat Laksour, just north of Place Bab Fteuh), offering super-stylish kaftans, and El Nour (57 Souikat Laksour), a non-profit organisation producing beautiful handmade traditional Moroccan embroidery, created by disadvantaged women and girls.

You'll also find some further interesting shops (and several beautiful riads) along Rue el Ksour (also known as Rue Laksour), which runs west off Souikat Laksour to Bab Laksour. These include Kif Kif and Kulchi, towards the western

*Traditional teapots*

end of the street offer chic clothing, souvenirs and handicrafts in contemporary Moroccan style.

## MOUASSINE MOSQUE

Back on the main drag north, proceed for about 300m/yds until the route widens in front of the **Mouassine Mosque** ❷ (closed to non-Muslims), constructed by the Saadian sultan Abdellah el Ghalib in 1562. It's one of the most impressive mosques in the medina, although it is difficult to appreciate from the outside, due to the clutter of shops built up around its walls. A number of these have roof terraces with views into the mosque's peaceful courtyards, although you will be expected to offer some kind of tip or payment in return, or buy something from the shop.

### Dar Cherifa

Situated just opposite the mosque, follow Derb Chorfa el Kebir (identified by a gold plaque reading 'Riad les Jardins de Mouassine') to **Dar Cherifa** ❸ (8 Derb Chorfa el Kebir; daily 8.30am–7pm; http://dar-cherifa.com), a magnificent house restored by Abdellatif Ait Ben Abdallah, a leading force in the authentic restoration of medina properties. You will need to knock to gain entry, but the welcome is warm. Its café-cum-library, see ❶, is a great space to enjoy a peaceful drink, as is its rooftop terrace, and it also hosts a lively programme of cultural events.

### Mouassine Fountain

Back on the main drag, walk past the mosque and turn immediately right. Dating from the 17th century, the **Mouassine Fountain** ❹ is just one of the eighty-odd public fountains that once dotted the medina, providing a public water supply for animal as well as human use. It's an impressively large structure, looking like the front of a miniature mosque with its three bays sheltered beneath a triple-arched facade, although the fountain itself is now dry.

## DYERS' SOUK

Just past the fountain is the **Dyers' Souk** ❺ (Souk Sebbaghine or Souk des Teinturiers), usually festooned with swathes of wool and silk, freshly dyed in vivid colours and hung out to dry above the street. A few dyers' workshops lie on either side; chemical dyes have replaced traditional plant dyes, but otherwise the process has barely changed for centuries.

## NORTH ALONG RUE MOUASSINE

Return to the Mouassine Fountain and turn right up Rue Mouassine. Close by is the **Bougainvillea Café**, see ❷, and further north, on the right-hand side of Rue Mouassine itself, is **Café Arabe** (see page 110), both decent options for lunch.

*Hand-shaped door knocker*

### Shrine of Sidi Abdelaziz

The northern stretch of Rue Mouassine, along with several others of the more important thoroughfares in the northern medina, is lined with ancient fondouks. These galleried lodging houses for traders and their animals are now given over to bazaars, storehouses or workshops, and sometimes used as sites in Marrakech's thriving film-location business.

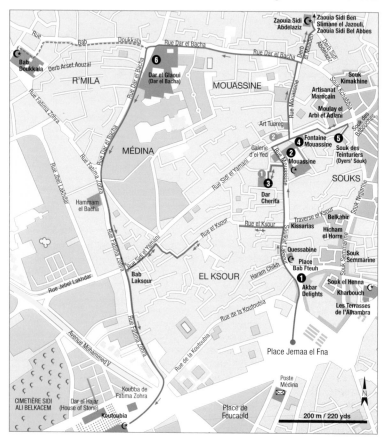

*The Bab Doukkala Mosque*                    *A dyers' workshop*

The street continues north to the **Zaouia Sidi Abdelaziz**, one of seven *zaouias* (each containing the tomb of a holy man or woman) that encircle the city. Two more – the **Zaouia Sidi Ben Slimane el Jazouli** and the **Zaouia Sidi Bel Abbes**, notable for its carved portal – lie further north. The *zaouias* are out of bounds to non-Muslims, and there are few reasons to venture further north, save for a few riads and restaurants that lie hidden in the residential maze.

### Dar el Bacha

Shortly before you reach the Zaouia Sidi Abdelaziz, Rue Dar el Bacha leads west towards Bab Doukkala. On the way it passes the sprawling **Dar el Bacha** ❻ (also known as Dar el Glaoui).

The palace originally belonged to the Glaoui, Berber overlords from the Atlas Mountains, who collaborated with the French during the Protectorate. The two brothers Thami and Madani Glaoui acquired vast wealth and influence: Thami was an acquaintance of Winston Churchill and attended the coronation of Elizabeth II.

After Morocco was granted Independence in 1956, the Glaoui were disgraced, and their properties seized by the state. The building briefly functioned as a museum but sadly is no longer open to the public, although you can get a sense of its scale and former splendour from the vast salmon-pink walls overlooking the road.

### Return to the Koutoubia

From here, if time allows, you could make a detour west along Rue Bab Doukkala, which bustles with local life, to the **Bab Doukkala Mosque**, with its own fine fountain.

From the Dar el Bacha turn left and head south down Rue Dar el Bacha until you join Rue Fatima Zohra, which eventually reaches the Koutoubia. En route is the **Bab Laksour**, leading to Rue el Ksour (see page 40), home to several interesting shops.

## Food and Drink

### ❶ DAR CHERIFA

8 Derb Chorfa el Kebir; tel: 0524-38 26 27; http://dar-cherifa.com; noon–7pm; €€

This café in this peaceful old historic riad serves juices, teas and good light lunches featuring a mix of Moroccan and European fare. Seating either in the courtyard or on the lovely roof terrace.

### ❷ BOUGAINVILLEA CAFE

33 Rue Mouassine; tel: 0524-44 11 11; 11am–10pm; €€

This colourful and convenient courtyard café (easy to spot next to the road junction near the Mouassine Mosque) serves up a nice selection of mainly Moroccan dishes, plus salads and sandwiches. Alternatively, just pop in for a coffee or mint tea with pastries. No alcohol.

*Café de France. Jemaa el Fna*

# THE SOUTHERN MEDINA

*This route explores the section of the southern medina closest to Jemaa el Fna, including the homes of two 19th-century viziers – the sumptuously decorated El Bahia Palace and Dar Si Said Museum – along with the engaging Maison Tiskiwin, home to a unique array of Berber crafts.*

**DISTANCE:** 2.5km (1.5 miles)
**TIME:** A half-day
**START:** Café de France, Jemaa el Fna
**END:** Jemaa el Fna
**POINTS TO NOTE:** For a longer itinerary you could combine this route with no. 5 (see page 49), spending the afternoon visiting El Badi Palace and the Saadian Tombs.

The southern part of the Marrakech medina is quite unlike the northern half. There are virtually no souks here (except-ing the jewellery souk, selling mainly modern gold, off Place des Ferblantiers). Instead, much of area is occupied by a string of magnificent palaces and man-sions including the El Bahia Palace and the beautiful Dar Si Said.

Heading slightly further south (cov-ered in route 5, see page 49) you will encounter the sprawling El Badi com-plex and the magical Saadian Tombs, located in the heart of the old fortified Kasbah.

## SETTING OFF

Start at **Café de France** ❶ (see page 33) on the eastern side of the Jemaa el Fna, then take Rue des Banques, a straight residential street to the left of the café as you face it. After a couple of minutes' walk bear right at a T-junction marked by a small sign for Hôtel Mounir, and after a couple more minutes, pass through an arch into the narrow **Rue Riad Zitoun el Jdid**. Despite its modest proportions, this street serves (improb-ably) as a busy traffic artery, particularly popular with speeding motorcyclists who whizz down the street with carefree abandon and making few allowances for pedestrians – especially dawdling foreigners. Watch your ankles.

## MAISON TISKIWIN

Walk down Rue Riad Zitoun el Jdid for about five minutes until you reach a nar-row alley (opposite the point at which the western side of the street opens up into a miniature square). A few steps down here is the beautiful **Mai-**

*Dar Si Said Museum*                               *Dar Si Said Museum interior*

son Tiskiwin ❷ (daily 9am–12.30pm, 2.30–6pm; charge). The home of Dutch anthropologist Bert Flint, this delightfully ramshackle old riad is stuffed with arts and crafts collected by Flint, including a superb collection of Berber textiles and pottery.

The collection – clothes, jewellery, headdresses, talismans, saddles and camel tack, carpets, domestic implements, weaponry and even a nomad's tent – traces the old Saharan trade routes from Marrakech to Timbuktu in Mali. The displays are supported by detailed explanations in French and maps pinpointing the location of the many and various tribes represented.

## DAR SI SAID MUSEUM

From Maison Tiskiwin, it's just a short hop north to the excellent **Dar Si Said Museum ❸** (daily except Thur 9am–5pm; charge). The museum occupies a particularly impressive riad, built in the 19th century by the brother of the Grand Vizier Ba Hmad, who was responsible for Palais Bahia (see page 46). Exhibits scattered around the labyrinthine ground floor include an impressive selection of Moroccan artefacts – ornate wooden doors and painted windows salvaged from southern kasbahs; old Qu'rans and antique leatherwork bags;

*El Bahia Palace*

## Medina living

Wandering through the medina can be a little like exploring a maze, yet clues can be gleaned, not just to daily activities, but also to beliefs, superstitions and traditions.

Doors are often works of art, impressively studded, sometimes with a smaller inner door (for humans), leaving the larger for heavy loads or donkeys. A potential gateway for *djinn* (demons), doors are often decorated with prophylactic symbols such as eyes, hands or geometric motifs. The knocker may be in the form of a hand (*khamsa*, meaning 'five'), representing the hand of Fatima, daughter of the Prophet, a symbol repeated many times in many different contexts.

Stacks of logs usually mean the presence of a baker or hammam, often both, for it is common for these places to share a furnace. You may see older children spinning yarn to make braid for kaftans (the ends of the thread are tied to buildings on street corners). Local butchers offer a *tangier*, an earthenware urn filled with different types of meat then placed on the communal fire.

Stalls selling candles, nougat and other sweets usually indicate the presence of a shrine (*zaouia*) centred on the tomb of a holy man or woman. Although these are visited all year round, a large gathering of people is likely to indicate a *moussem* (religious festival).

brightly coloured traditional clothes and fabrics.

Exhibits aside, it's the building itself that really captures the imagination. Twisting corridors eventually lead to a central courtyard, with a beautifully tiled fountain set beneath a painted wooden gazebo and gorgeously painted and tiled doors to all four sides. From here, steps lead up to the spectacularly decorated chambers above, with intricately tiled and painted ceilings and a selection of wedding palanquins and assorted carpets.

### EL BAHIA PALACE

Return to Rue Riad Zitoun el Jdid and turn left, past the large **Hammam Ziani**. On the left, at the end of the street, is **El Bahia Palace ❹** (daily 9am–4.45pm; charge), built in the 19th century to serve as the palace of Bou Ahmed Ben Moussa, grand vizier to Sultan Abdelaziz, whose disastrous rule (he was just 14 when he acceded to the throne) and chronic overspending led to the foreign occupation of Morocco under Moulay Hassan in 1912.

The Bahia (which translates as 'The Brilliant') was built at the public's expense over a period of six years in honour of Bou Ahmed's first wife – although it also accommodated three further wives and no fewer than 24 concubines. In total, the palace covers around 8 hectares (20 acres) and has a total of 150 rooms, only a fraction

*A quiet spot at El Bahia*                    *Palace wall tiles*

of which can be seen by the public –
a stunning display of the period's faux
Alhambra-style decoration, using the
very finest Moroccan craftsmen and
superior workmanship.

### Lavish decoration

The beautiful complex of cool recep-
tion rooms, courtyards and gardens,
which was seized by the royal family
on the restoration of the monarchy,
contains little in the way of furniture,
but the decoration is lavish, with *zellige*, *zawwaga* (wood painted with floral
patterns and arabesques) and carved
stucco. This is particularly so in the
first rooms, 'Le Petit Riad', where Bou
Ahmed received official visitors. These
rooms were used by the French Resident General during the protectorate.

This area leads you through to La
Petite Cour, with more rooms, and then
La Grande Cour, on the left-hand side
of which is the garden, and Le Grand
Riad (1866–7), which was the orig-
inal palace belonging to Si Moussa,
Bou Ahmed's father, and the quarters
of Lalla Zineb, Bou Ahmed's first wife.
Many celebrities have stayed here as
guests of the Moroccan royal family.

### The mellah

Behind the palace stretches the *mellah*, the old Jewish quarter, now home
to just a few Jewish families, but with a
definite Jewish character, with features
such as Stars of David on the doors
(see box).

## PLACE DES FERBLANTIERS

Return to the bottom of Rue Riad Zitoun
ed Jdid and head left, into the pedestri-
anised **Place des Ferblantiers** ❺ on
the edge of the *mellah*, famous for the
shops of its metalsmiths (ferblantiers),
piled high with ornate brass lanterns.

En route you pass the **Grande Bijouterie**, an arcade of goldsmiths crammed
with 24-carat gold jewellery including
heavy gold belts, filigree earrings and

### The mellah

The former Jewish quarters in Morocco's various medinas are collectively
known as the *mellah*, a word that means
'salt' and is thought to allude to the
Jews' domination of the salt trade in the
16th century, and in particular to their
job of draining and salting the heads
of decapitated rebels before they were
impaled on the gates of a city. The *mellah* was normally located close to the
royal palace to benefit from royal protec-
tion (on payment of a special tax).

Marrakech's *mellah* still contains ves-
tiges of its once-sizeable Jewish community, including a functioning synagogue,
occasional Hebrew signs and a large
Jewish cemetery on the quarter's eastern side. Traditionally, the city's goldsmiths were Jewish, and, to this day, one
of the main gold souks is situated off
Place des Ferblantiers, on the *mellah's*
western edge.

*Grande Bijouterie gold belts*

bracelets, a full set of which is traditionally given to a woman by her husband on marriage (rural brides are more likely to wear silver).

Until recent changes in family law, such gold was sometimes all that a woman was entitled to take as a divorce settlement. If you're shopping for gold here, note that the price of gold jewellery is governed by current global gold prices, which are posted in the shops, plus extra for the work. Negotiate on this basis.

If you'd prefer to stop for lunch, Place des Ferblantiers has several good places to eat, including **Kosybar**, see , and **Le Tanjia**, see ②, as well as various (touristy) sandwich shops and brochette stands.

If you want to visit El Badi Palace and the Saadian Tombs (see page 49), head through the arch on the south side of the square and turn right alongside the walls of the palace to the ticket office. Alternatively, you can return directly to the Jemaa el Fna along Rue Riad Zitoun el Kdim, passing the **Earth Café**, see ③, en route, which does a tasty tajine at rock-bottom prices.

## Food and Drink

### ① KOSYBAR

47 Place des Ferblantiers; tel: 0524-38 03 24; www.kosybar.com; 11am–1am; €€€
Excellent views over Place des Ferblantiers and of the neighbouring storks' nests from its rooftop terrace Lunch options here include well-made pasta and risotto, sushi and Moroccan classics with a modern twist. Has a good choice of alcoholic drinks – or just have a coffee or tea.

### ② LE TANJIA

14 Derb Jdid, between El Bahia Palace and Place des Ferblantiers; tel: 0524-38 38 36; noon–3pm and 8pm–midnight; €€
Le Tanjia's opulent interior, filled with divans and low tables, tends to fill up with tour groups, but the Moroccan food remains good, including classic dishes such as *pastilla* and some luxurious tajines (such as beef with hard-boiled eggs and almonds, and lamb with quinces). The service can be variable and belly dancers sometimes make an appearance, which may or not appeal, but the terrace is lovely at dusk.

### ③ EARTH CAFÉ

2 Derb Zawak, Riad Zitoun el Kedim; tel: 661-289 409; www.earthcafemarrakech.com; 11am–late; €
The Earth Café is something different in Marrakech: a 'vegetarian vegan' café serving deliciously different dishes amid the jewel-coloured walls of a narrow courtyard. Expect dishes such as filo stuffed with pepper, courgette and ricotta, or with spinach, pumpkin and goat's cheese in an orange confit sauce.

*El Badi Palace*

# EL BADI PALACE AND THE SAADIAN TOMBS

*Exploring the lower half of the southern medina, this route visits the ruined El Badi Palace and the magical Saadian Tombs before stopping for lunch in the Kasbah and, possibly, taking time out for some pampering at a hammam.*

---

**DISTANCE:** 2.5km (1.5 miles)
**TIME:** A half-day, or a full day if you want to spend the afternoon being pampered.
**START:** Jemaa el Fna
**END:** Rue de la Kasbah
**POINTS TO NOTE:** The Saadian Tombs can get busy by mid-morning, so start as early as you can. This route can be combined with route 4, but lunch followed by an afternoon in a spa may prove more tempting than such a full sightseeing programme.

---

The Saadian Tombs are among Marrakech's top sights, and are all the more enchanting for their setting half hidden in the shadow of the Kasbah Mosque. If you don't have time to do the whole of this route, a visit to the tombs should take precedence over El Badi.

### SETTING OFF

From the Jemaa el Fna (see page 32) take Rue Riad Zitoun el Kdim to Place des Ferblantiers, a straightforward 10-minute walk. Cross the square, go through the archway on the southern side, turn right and walk alongside the walls of El Badi Palace to the ticket booth and entrance.

### EL BADI PALACE

Sprawling south of Place des Ferblantiers is **El Badi Palace** ❶ (daily 9am–4.45pm; charge). The name means 'the incomparable', although the ruined complex is now more remarkable for its size than for its splendour.

The palace really comes into its own as a venue for evening entertainment. Concerts (from rock to classical) are regularly held here, and in June it is the setting for a folklore festival including a nightly fantasia – a dramatic display of horsemanship in which participants gallop towards each other, firing muskets into the air. For details of events check www.madein-marrakech.com.

Enclosed by massive crumbling walls, topped by precarious-looking storks' nests, El Badi was built by the great Saadian sultan El Mansour in

*The ruined palace complex*

the 16th century. Construction was financed by ransom money extracted from Portuguese nobles captured during battles, gold from the newly captured Songhai empire and profits from sugar production in the Souss Valley. According to contemporary accounts, El Mansour traded the sugar pound for pound for white Carrara marble from Italy, with which he covered the building, and imported elaborate furnishings all the way from China.

The palace took 25 years to build and was famously beautiful, its pavilions, towers and galleries impressing many a foreign ambassador. Sadly, it was short-lived: in 1683, Moulay Ismail, the second sultan of the current Alaouite dynasty, destroyed the palace over the course of just 12 years, stripping its marble to furnish his own vast palace in Meknes, the new imperial capital.

Small patches of dusty *zellige* (mosaic tiling) can be seen here and there, but the most notable features today are the vast central courtyard and what remains of its once-famous sunken gar-

dens, ingeniously irrigated by pools fed by meltwater from the Atlas Mountains.

It's also worth climbing the palaces great walls of El Badi (access on the northern side), from where there are lovely views over the storks' nests, the medina's rooftops, the minaret of the Kasbah Mosque and, in winter, the snow-capped Atlas Mountains.

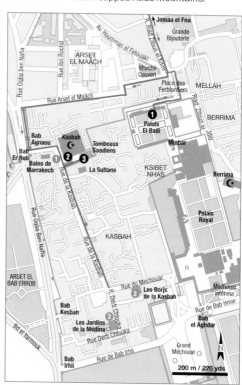

*The tomb complex*                    *The Kasbah Mosque's minaret*

### The Koutoubia's minbar

Perhaps to draw more visitors to this rather bleak ruin, the spectacular **minbar** (moveable pulpit from which the imam leads the prayers and delivers sermons) of the Koutoubia Mosque (see page 30) is housed in a pavilion on the southwest corner of the courtyard. Intricately crafted in Córdoba in around 1120 for the Almoravid forerunner of the current Koutoubia Mosque, it is a masterpiece of Islamic art that took Andalusian craftsmen eight years to complete. The workmanship involved in the marquetry decoration of the staircase – no two panels are exactly the same – shows something of the splendour of Marrakech during the 12th century. In use in the Koutoubia until 1962, it was wheeled out on Fridays; the imam ascended only to the middle step in submission to God and the Prophet Mohammed.

### THE KASBAH

Leaving El Badi, retrace your route to Place des Ferblantiers and continue in a westerly direction along Rue Arset el Maâch. At the bottom of the street cut left through an arch, head through two further arches (you are now passing between the Kasbah's double walls) and then turn left, leaving the handsome city gate, Bab Agnaou (see page 65), on your right. The route leads towards the **Kasbah Mosque** ❷ (Mosquée de la Kasbah; closed to non-Muslims), which,

## Hammams

The Kasbah area has several upmarket spas, some in riad-style hotels. Expect to pay from about 180DH for a hammam including a body scrub up to 2,000DH for full-day packages including several treatments, and book in advance.

Les Bains de Marrakech (2 Derb Sedra, Bab Agnaou, Kasbah; tel: 0524-38 14 28; www.lesbainsdemarrakech.com; daily 9am–7.30pm). Marrakech's most sublime spa experience: floaty curtains, white divans scattered with rose petals and moody lighting create a sensual setting for an extensive range of treatments.

Les Borjs de la Kasbah (Rue du Méchouar (off the southern end of Rue de la Kasbah); tel: 0524-38 11 01; www.lesborjs delakasbah.com; times vary). L'Arganier Spa at the small riad-style Les Borjs de la Kasbah hotel features an impressive, marble-clad hammam and a relaxing treatment area.

Les Jardins de la Medina (21 Rue Derb Chtouka; tel: 0524-38 18 51; www.les jardinsdelamedina.com; daily 8.30am–8.30pm). This smart riad at the southern end of the Kasbah has a small but well-run spa with massages, wraps, facials and packages.

La Sultana (403 Rue de la Kasbah; tel: 0524-38 80 08; www. lasultanahotels. com/marrakech; daily 10am–10pm). Offers treatments from traditional Moroccan massages with Argan oil and black soap to four-hand massages.

*El Badi ruins*

like Bab Agnaou, was originally built by the Almohads and is thus contemporary with the Koutoubia Mosque (see page 30). However, its minaret – although topped by three brass spheres like the Koutoubia – is modest by comparison, and the mosque has been remodelled several times.

The kasbah (pronounced 'ksiba') is the stronghold of an Arab city, and in Marrakech it protects the seat of power – the Royal Palace (Palais Royal) and Dar el Makhzen (House of Government; see page 64).

### The Saadians

When the Saadian dynasty burst on to the scene in the 16th century, Morocco was in a feeble state. Anarchy had taken hold during the Wattasid dynasty, and the Portuguese controlled several Atlantic ports. Rising up from the Draa valley, in southern Morocco, the Saadians united supporters in the name of jihad, first basing themselves in Taroudant and then, in 1525, from their seat in Marrakech. They were the first Arab – rather than Berber – dynasty to seize power since the Idrissids in the 8th century.

Under Ahmed El Mansur el Dehbi, 'the Victorious and Golden', their imperialist ambitions turned south, particularly to the gold-rich Songhai empire on the banks of the Niger, conquered by El Mansur in 1591.

### The Saadian Tombs

As you turn right into the broad area in front of the Kasbah Mosque, where a few souvenir stalls have taken root, you will see a sign for the **Saadian Tombs** ❸ (Tombeaux Saadiens; Rue de la Kasbah; daily 9am–4.45pm; charge), the cemetery of the Saadian sultans and their entourages.

Accessed via a slender passage on the corner of the mosque, the tombs were sealed off by the tyrannical Moulay Ismail in the 17th century and were gradually forgotten until the early 20th century, when they were spotted on aerial photographs taken by the French.

Set around a garden, the complex contains 66 members of the Saadian dynasty plus the tombs of numerous retainers. The central mausoleum is known as the Hall of Twelve Columns; as you enter, the tomb of Ahmed el Mansour (1578–1603), who built El Badi Palace, is in the middle on the left, flanked by the tombs of his son and grandson. Fine *zellige* (mosaic tiling) work, intricately carved stucco and slender pillars supporting a spectacular cedar dome with the stalactite carving that is characteristic of Saadian architecture, provide a sumptuous yet elegant setting. To the left of the Hall of Twelve Columns is the prayer hall containing the graves of Alaouite princes from the 18th century.

On the other side of the cemetery another structure, with an ornate

*Saadian Tombs detail*                    *Saadian Tombs*

Andalusian-style entrance, contains the tombs of Mohammed ech Sheik, founder of the Saadians; Sultan Abdallah el Ghallib, who expanded the Ben Youssef Madrassa (see page 37); and Lala Messaouda, Ahmed El Mansour's mother.

A lunch option across the road from the tombs is **Nid' Cigogne**, see ❶.

### Rue de la Kasbah

From the Saadian Tombs, **Rue de la Kasbah** leads south to Rue du Méchouar, named after the parade ground of the Royal Palace and Dar el Makhzen (see page 64). A lively north–south thoroughfare, Rue de la Kasbah is worth a wander. At the start, near the tombs, look for the **Centre Artisanal** (a government-run shop selling fixed-price handicrafts). Even if you prefer to bargain in the souks, it's worth popping in to get an idea of prices beforehand.

### Lunch and a spa option

If you fancy lunch by a pool, there are several nice riads in the Kasbah area, including **Les Borjs de la Kasbah** in Rue du Méchouar, see ❷, and, nearby, **Les Jardins de la Medina**, see ❸ (both have spas). There are also several kebab stands on Rue de la Kasbah. These can be good: a queue of locals will indicate if this is the case.

Having spent the morning sightseeing, you may wish to reward yourself with an indulgent afternoon in a spa (see box on Hammams).

## Food and Drink

### ❶ NID' CIGOGNE

60 Place des Tombeaux Saadiens; tel: 0524-38 20 92; 9am–9pm; €€

Serves salads, sandwiches, omelettes and basic couscous and tajines, but is best for its terrace views over the Kasbah Mosque and the storks' nests that crown the Kasbah's walls.

### ❷ LES BORJS DE LA KASBAH

Rue du Méchouar; tel: 0524-38 11 01; www.lesborjsdelakasbah.com; lunch 12.30–2pm, dinner 8–11pm; €€

Riad-style hotel offering a good selection of Moroccan and French dishes. You can order a simple lunch by the pool (with free use of the pool included) or a more elaborate meal on the central patio in the adjacent Le Jasmin restaurant.

### ❸ LES JARDINS DE LA MEDINA

21 Derb Chtouka; tel: 0524-38 18 51; www.lesjardinsdelamedina.com; lunch noon–2.30pm, dinner 5.30–10.30pm; €€€

One of Marrakech's top-rated restaurants, offering a range of French, Moroccan and Mediterranean food served next to the pool (although unfortunately the pool itself can only be used if you're staying at the hotel).

*Place de la Liberté*

# GUELIZ

*Although lacking in specific sights, the Ville Nouvelle (New Town) has wide boulevards, parks, chic cafés and smart boutiques, which make a refreshing change from the medina. This route takes a stroll along and around its main artery, Avenue Mohammed V.*

**DISTANCE:** 3km (2 miles)
**TIME:** A half day
**START:** Koutoubia Mosque
**END:** Place Abdel Moumen Ben Ali
**POINTS TO NOTE:** This route, which includes opportunities for shopping, is best suited to the morning. If you want to extend it into the afternoon, you could add the Majorelle Garden (see page 58), a 10-minute walk from Place Abdel Moumen Ben Ali.

Marrakech's Ville Nouvelle offers a change of scenery from the crowds of the medina, as well as a snapshot of modern Moroccan life – urbane, cosmopolitan and glamorous in places. Heart of the new town is Guéliz, home to numerous shops, restaurants and tour operators, as well as a selection of small- and medium-size hotels (see page 105). Bus no.1 runs between Place de Foucauld and Place Abdel Moumen Ben Ali (from the first bus stand on Place de Foucauld, opposite the Koutoubia). A taxi should cost about 20–30DH.

### A place apart

Guéliz was laid out in the early 20th century by French architect Henri Prost. As with Morocco's other French-built cities, it was set well apart from the medina, in keeping with a decree of General Lyautey (see page 56), the first Resident General. Although an arch colonialist, he believed in preserving rather than erasing local culture. This approach led to the increasing isolation and economic backwardness of the Morrocan medinas during the colonial era, but ultimately ensured their long-term survival and preservation.

The French colonial influence, including striking examples of Art Deco, is still evident in much of Guéliz's architecture, although the district's original character is being slowly eroded by the taste for more contemporary Arabian-style buildings, with soaring marble lobbies and great expanses of tinted plate glass.

### THE MAIN ARTERY

Guéliz is divided by **Avenue Mohammed V**, a long boulevard marked by the

*The Cyber Parc*

Koutoubia (see page 30) at one end and a small range of hills, the 'Guéliz', topped by the walls of an old French fort, at the other. In between, apartment and office blocks in the now obligatory pink sandstone flank either side. The walk from the Koutoubia on Place de Foucauld to Place Abdel Moumen Ben Ali, the hub of the New Town, is a popular route for promenading *Marrakshis* in the early evening.

### Bab Nkob and Cyber Parc

Begin the walk between the two halves of the city at the **Koutoubia ❶**. Leave the medina by **Bab Nkob ❷**, a broad breach in the city walls rather than an actual gate, and head along the avenue.

On the left, just before Bab Nkob, is the **Cyber Parc Moulay Abdeslam**, a garden planted with olive, mimosa, acacia and fig trees, and with a café, auditorium and free WiFi hotspots, a public initiative of Maroc Telecom.

### Catholic church

Over the next big junction, **Place de la Liberté**, take the second left, Rue de Imam de Ali, down to a little Catholic church, **Eglise des Saints Martyrs**, built in the 1930s and now attracting a mainly West African congregation. You may be able to gain access to the church if the caretaker's around – try knocking on the door to the left of the main entrance.

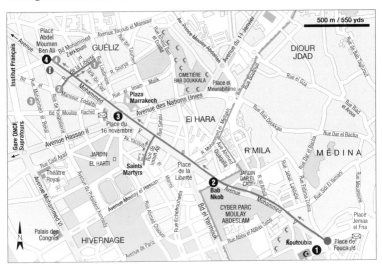

*Guéliz street scene*

### Place du 16 novembre

Return to Mohammed V and head a little further on to **Place du 16 novembre ❸**, which commemorates the day Mohammed V returned from exile in 1955, and is dominated by the main post office.

On the opposite side of this intersection is the glitzy **Plaza Marrakech** shopping mall, full of fast-food outlets, cafes and upmarket shops.

---

## The French protectorate

In the 'scramble for Africa', the great land grab by European powers at the end of the 19th century, Morocco was one of the last countries to be claimed. An independent Islamic country for over 1,000 years, with a strong tribal structure and dynastic government, it wasn't considered an easy country to colonise. However, French loans to the weak and profligate Sultan Abdelaziz (1894–1908) led to increasing European encroachment, and in 1912 the Treaty of Fez made Morocco a 'protectorate' of Spain and France. Spain gained the poorer north and the Spanish Sahara, and France gained 'useful Morocco', as General Lyautey, the first Resident General, liked to call it. While Spain was a neglectful colonial master, France set about modernising its territory, developing agriculture and industry and building roads, ports and a railway.

---

### Luxury on Liberté

A few blocks further north, Mohammed V crosses **Rue de la Liberté**, a smart street harbouring several of the city's more exclusive shops. On the right-hand side of the junction you may notice small groups of waiting women – casual maids hoping, often in vain, to be hired for the day.

Close to here, Yahya Création (61 Rue de Yougoslavie, Shop 49–50; www.yahya-group.com) showcases a spectacular selection of traditional lamps. Rue de la Liberté's shops display a more restrained side to Moroccan design than the exuberant bazaars of the medina.

Along the right leg, **Scènes du Lin** (no. 70) sells cushions, throws, tablecloths, glassware, and richly coloured fabrics by the metre. Close by are several upmarket jewellers and *traiteurs*; and the exclusive **Secrets de Marrakech** spa (no. 62). One of the city's best commercial art galleries, **Matisse** (www.matisse-art gallery. com) is at no. 61.

Liberté's left leg offers more luxury shops, including, on the corner with Mohammed V, **Place Vendôme** (leather bags and saddles) and, next door, the Belgian chocolate shop, **Jeff de Bruges** (no. 17), which sells delicious, fairly traded chocolates and ice creams. Further along the street, **L'Orientaliste** (nos 11 and 15) offers a range of hefty antique furniture and oversized ceramics.

*Café in Guéliz*

### Refreshment options

For a late breakfast or early lunch in the area, try **Café du Livre**, see ❶, on Rue Tarik ibn Ziad. **Kechmara**, see ❷, is a stylish restaurant-bar on Rue de la Liberté. If you just want a coffee and a sit down, **Amandine**, see ❸, on Rue Mohammed el Bekkal, is one of the best patisseries in town.

### Centre point

Return to Mohammed V and head a little further north to the busy Place **Abdel Moumen Ben Ali** ❹, where the terrace of **Café les Négociants**, see ❹, is a well-loved vantage point. Also here is the **National Tourist Office** (Office National de Tourisme; see page 130).

The only reasons for venturing further north are to book tickets at the Supratours office or the railway station (both on Avenue Hassan II), or to visit the Majorelle Garden (see page 58), a 15-minute wak away on Boulevard Mohammed Zerktouni and Avenue Yacoub el Mansour.

---

## Food and Drink

### ❶ CAFÉ DU LIVRE

44 Rue Tarik ibn Ziad; tel: 0524-43 21 49; 9.30am–9pm, closed Sun; €€
Marrakech's first and only literary café, popular with expats and serving tasty breakfasts, lunches and light dinners – salads, sandwiches and bistro fare, backed up by a good drinks selection and proper pots of tea. Also offers free WiFi (and hence the name) an interesting library of books to browse.

### ❷ KECHMARA

3 Rue de la Liberté; tel: 0524-42 25 32; www.kechmara.ma; 7.30am–midnight, food served noon–11pm; €€
Fashionable international restaurant in the heart of the Ville Nouvelle. Always packed at lunchtime on the roof terrace and in the evening, when there's a DJ most nights. Good-value lunchtime set menus.

### ❸ AMANDINE

17 Rue Mohammed el Bekal; tel: 0524-44 96 12; www.amandinemarrakech.com; 7am–9pm; €
A favourite patisserie-cum-ice cream parlour with a tiled interior and potted palms. Ideal for morning coffee or afternoon tea with choice French cakes or sticky oriental sweets. Closed at lunchtime. No alcohol.

### ❹ CAFÉ LES NÉGOCIANTS

Place Abdel Moumen Ben Ali; 0524-43 57 82; www.cafe-lesnegociants.com; 6am–11pm; €
Secure a table (not always easy) on the large wrap-around terrace and watch the passing scene over orange juice, coffee and croissants or a simple mint tea. Highly professional old-school waiters. No alcohol.

*The Majorelle Garden*

# MAJORELLE GARDEN AND THE PALMERAIE

*This route visits a dramatic garden designed in the 1920s by the painter Jacques Majorelle, then continues to the Palmeraie, an ancient date plantation that has become Marrakech's address-of-choice for the city's rich and famous.*

**DISTANCE:** 6km (3.75 miles)
**TIME:** A half-day or longer if you want to play golf or go horse-riding at the Palmeraie Golf Palace
**START:** Majorelle Garden
**END:** Palmeraie Golf Palace
**POINTS TO NOTE:** This route is best undertaken mid-afternoon, when the heat and light have mellowed.

The Majorelle Garden is a straightforward walk east from Place Abdel Moumen Ben Ali in Guéliz. To reach the outlying Palmeraie, you'll need transport, however. A calèche is the most romantic way to visit; although a taxi is quicker and about a quarter of the price (around 40–50DH each way).

## MAJORELLE GARDEN

The impressive **Majorelle Garden** ❶ (Jardin Majorelle; Avenue Yacoub el Mansour; www.jardinmajorelle.com; May–Sept 8am–6pm, Oct–April until 5.30pm; charge) is one of the city's top attractions.

### Jacques Majorelle

The Majorelle Garden was designed by the French painter Jacques Majorelle (1886–1962) in the 1920s and restored by the fashion designer Yves Saint Laurent and his partner Pierre Bergé during the 1980s. The son of the French furniture-maker, Louis Majorelle (known for his exquisite, internationally acclaimed, Art Nouveau designs), Jacques first visited Marrakech in 1917 to recuperate from an illness at the suggestion of General Lyautey (see page 56), French Morocco's first Resident General and a family friend.

By this time the painter had already travelled widely in Egypt, but it was Marrakech that held his fascination. He first used the city as a springboard for forays into the Atlas Mountains and Sahara desert, then in 1924 he purchased a plot of land on the edge of the French quarter and constructed Villa Bou Saf-Saf in the local style.

He later commissioned the architect Paul Sinclair to build a separate studio (now the Museum of Islamic Arts) in a neo-Mauresque style; it was the first

*Spiky succulents in the garden*

structure in the garden to be painted cobalt blue, a colour Majorelle had been mesmerised by in the Atlas, where it is used extensively.

The garden took shape over a period of nearly 40 years, with plants sourced from all over the world. Although Majorelle was a painter, the garden, which first opened to the public as early as 1947, is said to be his greatest work.

Tragically, he did not end his days here: following a car accident, he returned to France, and died shortly afterwards.

### The garden

Spiky succulents and palms, towering bamboos and giant ferns are set off by brilliant cobalt-blue pavilions, terracotta paths and pots, and splashes of hibiscus and bougainvillea tumbling over walls and other verticals. The drenched colours and graphic shapes evoke a painting by the French Post-Impressionist Paul Gauguin; the shady pools and other water features add to the garden's elemental, faintly disturbing feel.

### Berber Museum

The Musée Berbère (extra charge for this) opened inside the gardens in 2012, replacing the Museum of Islamic Arts, which formerly stood here. Housed in Majorelle's former garden studio, the museum showcases the collection of Berber crafts and artefacts amassed by Pierre Bergé and Yves Saint Laurent over the years. Exhibits include superb sets of traditional Berber jewellery, weaving and metalwork, plus clothes, textiles and wood-carvings, all decorated with characteristically bold geometric designs. There are also a dozen or so of Jacques Majorelle's paintings of kasbahs in the Middle and High Atlas. On the wall in the last room is a poster advertising the 'Grand Atlas', one of several designed by Majorelle for a campaign to promote tourism in the 1920s.

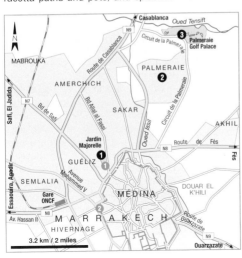

*The Palmeraie Golf Palace*

Next to the museum, is a courtyard café, see ❶, that serves drinks and light refreshments. Another option for a pit-stop is **Café Glacier Snack Reda**, see ❷, five minutes' walk down the road.

### THE PALMERAIE

The **Palmeraie ❷**, a wealthy area of palatial properties, lies off the Route de Fès on the northeast side of Marrakech, about 5km (3 miles) from the centre or 3km (2 miles) from the Majorelle Garden. This neighbourhood is the home and playground of the city's rich and famous, who are numerous, and expensive villas and hotels set in luxuriant gardens abound.

According to legend, this ancient palm grove marks the camp of the invading Almohads in the 12th century and is the legacy of the soldiers' discarded date stones. This suggests a lush oasis, but the reality is a rather thin, disappointing landscape of stooping palms (watered by ancient artesian wells), mud walls and dusty roads.

Nevertheless, a visit in the late afternoon, when the light softens the harshness of the landscape, is a pleasant prospect. Scattered among the mansions are several upmarket hotels and restaurants, including the opulent **Palmeraie Golf Palace ❸** (see page 106). Among its luxurious facilities (open to non-residents) are tennis courts, a superb golf course (see page 23), stables where horses can be hired by the hour or half-day, and **Nikki Beach**, a super-fashionable day club with a hip Ibiza-meets-St Tropez atmosphere.

This is also a good place to go camel riding, with plenty of brightly saddled dromedaries for hire, offering short walks amidst the palms. Be sure to negotiate a price in advance and be prepared to bargain hard – starting prices are usually on the high side.

## Food and Drink

### ❶ MAJORELLE GARDEN

Avenue Yacoub el Mansour;
tel: 0524-30 18 52; 8am–5pm;
€€
The Majorelle Garden's secluded café has an attractive courtyard with wrought-iron chairs and parasols. There's a good range of hot and cold drinks (including an extensive range of teas and fresh juices), while food options consist mainly of light meals including brochettes, soups, salads and daily specials.

### ❷ CAFÉ GLACIER SNACK REDA

Avenue Yacoub el Mansour; no tel.;
8am–10pm; €
Just a short walk from the Majorelle Garden, this simple, inexpensive, local favourite offers outdoor seating and a range of basic tasty grills and salads. Try the chicken brochettes, which are especially tasty.

*Menara gardens and pavilion*

# THE MENARA

*A gentle jaunt to the Menara offers one of Marrakech's classic calèche rides. After a walk around the gardens, return via La Mamounia, the country's most famous hotel, returned to its original splendour after a three-year revamp, with stunning traditional Moroccan décor added to its original Art Deco design.*

**DISTANCE:** 4.5km (2.75 miles)
**TIME:** 2 hours
**START:** Place de Foucauld or another calèche station
**END:** La Mamounia Hotel
**POINTS TO NOTE:** If you don't want to take a calèche or taxi to the Menara, you can walk here from the Bab Jdid, which is east of the Koutoubia, in about 20 minutes, or take bus (no. 11) from Place de Foucauld. The Menara is also a stop on the hop-on, hop-off Marrakech Bus Touristique (www.alsa. ma/fr/bus-touristique). Dress smart for La Mamounia.

One of the attractions of the Menara gardens is the classic view of the central pavilion framed by the snow-capped Atlas Mountains. However, this truly stunning vista is only possible to enjoy on a clear winter or spring day (usually November–May), as in summer and autumn the mountains are not only snowless but also usually obscured by a dusty haze.

If conditions are right, the gardens are well worth a late-afternoon or sunset visit. To get here, hire a calèche at any of the calèche ranks: Place de Foucauld (see page 31) always has plenty. Be prepared to bargain like crazy and aim for a fare of around 150DH per hour for the entire calèche. If you intend to spend long in the gardens, you might prefer to hire a calèche in one direction only to save paying extra for it to wait around during your visit.

## Food and Drink

**❶ TANZANIA**
Kawkab Centre, Avenue Moulay el Hassan I; tel: 0524-43 27 88; dinner 7.30pm–1am; €€€€
For an early evening cocktail, you could try Tanzania, a vast, African Jungle-themed open-air restaurant-bar in the Kawkab Centre – although the live music (soul, jazz, funk), for which it's best known, doesn't get going until 10.30pm.

*La Mamounia*

## THE MENARA

The **Menara** 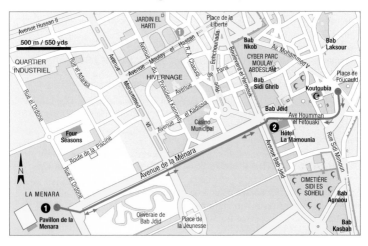 (Avenue de la Menara; daily 5.30am–6.30pm) was established by the Almohads in the 12th century to provide agricultural produce for the sultan and for profit. In the 16th century the Saadians added a summer pavilion where the courtiers could catch the cooling mountain breezes, although it was remodelled by the Alaouite Sultan Abderrahmane in 1869.

Ascend the pavilion's staircase (entrance on the south side; charge) to see its painted ceiling and for views over the great square basin, measuring 800m (875yds) in perimeter and 2m (6ft) deep. As well as vistas of the Atlas (assuming favourable weather conditions) the pavilion also offers fine views over the great plain of Marrakech, a sea of olive trees to the fore and the Koutoubia rising in the distance. Afterwards, stroll in the olive groves and enjoy a mint tea in the small café behind the far side of the pool.

## LA MAMOUNIA

On the way back to town it's worth stopping off at the city's landmark hotel, **La Mamounia** ❷ (see page 105), for a drink or a bite to eat – you will pass it on your return along Avenue Bab Jdid. Alternatively, dip further into the Hivernage area, where cafés and ice-cream parlours are interspersed among the big hotels. The Kawkab Centre on Avenue Moulay el Hassan I has several interesting possibilities, including **Tanzania**, see ❶, a hip restaurant-bar.

*Early morning at Bab Ghmat*

# TOUR OF THE GATES

*Marrakech is encircled by some 16km (10 miles) of red sandstone walls punctuated by a dozen gates, best appreciated by taking a tour in one of the city's old-fashioned calèches. This trip is particularly lovely in the evening, when the gates and walls are illuminated.*

---

**DISTANCE:** 16km (10 miles)
**TIME:** 2 hours
**START:** Place de Foucauld
**END:** Place de Foucauld
**POINTS TO NOTE:** This ride is likely to cost around 250DH (more with stops), but be sure to negotiate the fare before you set off.

---

One of the longer calèche rides, the complete 'tour des remparts' proceeds clockwise from **Place de Foucauld ❶**, passing by the more important gates en route. If you prefer to sample just a section of the fortifications, your driver will probably suggest you combine a tour of the leafy Hivernage area (see page 62) with a trot past the western walls to the Royal Palace.

### HISTORY OF THE WALLS

The walls of Marrakech have fallen and risen at various times in the city's history. They were first laid out by the Almoravids as defence against the invading Almohads. Originally there were some 20 gates in total, but many are now bricked up or incorporated into dwellings, with only about half that number still functioning as entrance and exit points. On your way around, notice the holes that pierce large sections of the walls and gates, many of them now crumbling and inhabited by nesting birds. These look like loopholes through which weapons could have been fired, but were in fact designed to provide an ingenious type

---

## Food and Drink

### ❶ LES JARDINS DE LA KOUTOUBIA

26 Rue de la Koutoubia; tel: 0524-38 88 00; www.lesjardinsdelakoutoubia.com; lunch noon–3.30pm, dinner 8.30–10.30pm; €€€€

For a treat spend a few hours at this swanky five-star hotel. Go for a cocktail in the Ouarazi piano bar (late afternoon–midnight), followed by a candlelit dinner in one of its restaurants, such as the superb Indian/Asian Les Jardins de Bala.

*The Agdal Gardens*

## Calèches

Calèches are one of the symbols of pleasure-loving Marrakech. These lovely carriages, with their great folding hoods and brass lamps, are a pleasure to behold, and the clip-clop of hooves is undeniably romantic, especially on a warm summer night. Concern for the horses deters some tourists, although the industry is better regulated than it once was, and most of the animals are in good condition. The drivers are required to have two sets of horses, so that one can rest while the other is working, and the issuing of licences is dependent on horses undergoing regular veterinary inspections.

Calèches can be hailed for a short journey, much like taxis, although drivers don't like going into the narrower streets of the medina, where manoeuvring may be a problem. It is more common to hire one for an excursion or for half a day to visit several sights.

The route and price should be agreed in advance: 150DH per hour for the entire calèche (not per person, as some driver may try to insist) is a good rule of thumb, although you'll probably have to bargain fairly hard to get this. Calèche ranks are found on Place de Foucauld, between the Jemaa el Fna and the Koutoubia, and outside the larger hotels. The carriages can take up to five passengers, with one on top with the driver.

of air-conditioning system, allowing refreshing breezes to blow through the walls into the city within.

Your calèche driver will probably tell you the names of the more notable gates as you reach them, but look out for (clockwise from north) **Bab el Khemis** ❷ (Thursday Gate – named after a Thursday market that has long taken place here) and **Bab Dbagh** ❸, both with finely carved façades, and **Bab Ghmat** ❹, through which the Almohads entered when capturing the city in 1147, reputedly using starving Christian mercenaries to fling open the portals. Just opposite is the **Zaouia Sidi Youssef Ben Ali**, a shrine to one of Marrakech's 'seven saints'.

### ROYAL PALACE

Skirting the cemetery, the route reaches the southern end of the medina and the **Bab Ahmar** ❺ (Red Gate), which serves as the entrance to the massive **Royal Palace** (Palais Royal) and **Dar el Makhzen** ❻ (House of Government). The external part of the complex comprises three linked *méchouars* (parade grounds), big enough to provide marching space for 22,000 soldiers. Today the palace is used mainly for state occasions (Mohammed VI has a smaller palace on Rue Sidi Mimoun, on the western side of the medina).

Opposite the palace are the **Agdal Gardens** ❼ (Jardins de l'Agdal), an agricultural estate established by the Almo-

*Calèche ride*                                                            *Bab Agnaou*

hads that still provides fruit for the royal household.

## WESTERN GATES

Returning north towards the Jemaa el Fna, the route goes through **Bab Irhli** ❽, then alongside the Kasbah's **Bab Kasbah** ❾ and through the double portal of **Bab er Rob** ❿, before reaching **Bab Agnaou** ⓫, with its beautifully carved concentric arches in blue-grey stone, originally built by the Almohads and subsequently remodelled in the 19th century.

From here the route returns to Place de Foucauld, although you could ask to detour via **Bab Jdid** ⓬ (New Gate), where La Mamounia (see page 62) would make a suitably spectacular end to this tour. Another upmarket possibility for food and drinks is **Les Jardins de la Koutoubia**, see ❶.

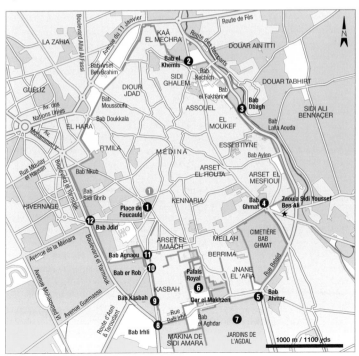

# ESSAOUIRA

*The laidback coastal town of Essaouira, 176km (110 miles) west of Marrakech, makes an ideal escape from the latter's heat and crowds. Specific sights are relatively thin on the ground, but the town's picture-perfect white-washed medina is one of the country's most attractive.*

**DISTANCE:** 3km (2 miles)

**TIME:** One day (ideal stay: 2–3 days)

**START:** Place Moulay Hassan

**END:** Essaouira beach

**POINTS TO NOTE:** The easiest and cheapest way to get from Marrakech to Essaouira is by bus. CTM buses run from the main Marrakech bus station (most services depart in the morning), while Supratours runs four coach services daily from the Supratours station (tel: 0524-47 53 17) on Avenue Hassan II, next to the railway station, in Guéliz. Tickets cost 75DH one way; Supratours tickets should ideally be booked at least a day in advance, or longer if you're travelling on a weekend; for CTM buses advance booking isn't normally needed. Alternatively, travel by grand taxi: a place in a shared taxi will cost about 100DH, or you can charter your own vehicle for around 800DH one way. Cars are not permitted inside Essaouira's medina, so you will need to find and pay for parking outside the walls if you decide to travel by hire car.

The journey from Marrakech to Essaouira takes around 3 hours by bus or *grand taxi* or about two hours by hire car. The road crosses the Haouz Plain, offering distant views of the Atlas on clear days, although otherwise there's little to see apart from a string of modern settlements and dusty fields.

As you draw near to Essaouira, you may see argan trees growing by the roadside. Source of a valuable oil (see page 96), these scrubby, thorny trees are reputed to grow only in southwest Morocco and Mexico.

## ON ARRIVAL

Essaouira has expanded far beyond its neat whitewashed medina, but most development is north of the town, leaving the old fortified harbour, still the hub of a thriving fishing industry, intact at the head of a fine 5km (3 mile) beach. Most accommodation is in riad-style hotels in the medina, although some modern establishments – including a prominent Sofitel – are starting to encroach along the bay.

*Gulls in Essaouira*

The main bus station is north of town, a 500m walk from Bab Doukkala (around 15DH by taxi from the centre); **Supratours buses** arrive just south of the medina off Avenue Lalla Aicha near Bab Marrakech.

## PLACE MOULAY HASSAN AND THE HARBOUR

A good place to start is the spacious, windswept **Place Moulay Hassan** ❶, fringed with attractive cafes on its

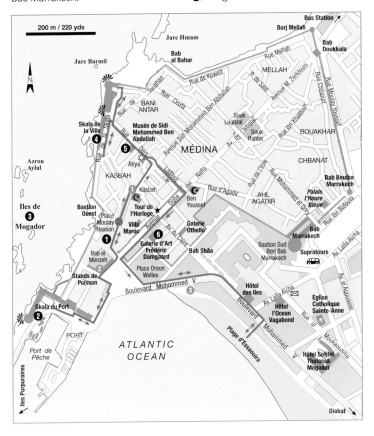

*In the woodworking souk*

northern side including the florid Casa Vera. A great place for breakfast near here is **Pâtisserie Driss**, see ❶. On the south side of the square are one of Essaouira's main eating attractions – the grilled fish stalls *(grillades)*, lined up under blue-and-white awnings, see ❷.

### The harbour

Past the fish stalls is the town's colourful harbour, particularly lively in the afternoons when the fishing boats bring in their catch. The port is enclosed in one of Essaouira's two surviving sec-

---

## Gnaoua Music Festival

Essaouira's Gnaoua Festival (www. festival-gnaoua.net), which takes place over a long weekend in late June, is one of the highlights in world music's calendar of festivals. Inaugurated in 1998, it now attracts more than 200,000 people, mainly Moroccans, but also an increasing number of foreigners, as knowledge of the event spreads. Rooted in the music of the *Gnaoua*, a black African sect descended from slaves introduced to Morocco in the 11th century, it includes elements of West African and Sufi trance music and also mixes in jazz and blues. Events, which are free, take place in Place Moulay Hassan, Bab Marrakech and on the beach. If you do manage to attend, expect a fairly unorthodox experience, with some members of the audience entering into trancelike states.

---

tions of ramparts, the **Skala du Port** ❷, dating from the 1770s, with a pair of squat rectangular towers at either end and a delicate neoclassical gateway in the middle. An Arabic inscription above the gateway records the fact that the ramparts were designed, incongruously, by an English renegade known locally as Ahmed el Inglizi (also known as Ahmed el Alj). El Inglizi appears to have originally been a member of the infamous Salé Rovers pirate clan, and is also thought to have worked as an architect and engineer in Rabat, although his original identity remains unknown. For a small fee you can walk along the ramparts (daily 9am–5.30pm; charge) and climb one of the towers for sweeping views of town and coast.

### Iles de Mogador

A short distance out to sea, directly opposite the harbour, lies a cluster of islands, formerly known as the Iles Purpuraires, now christened the **Iles de Mogador** ❸. In ancient times these islands, like many other such places around the Mediterranean, were a base for the manufacture of a purple dye known as Tyrian purple. The dye, derived from the murex shellfish, was very much in demand in 1st-century Rome to create the distinctive stripe on the senators' togas. The islands also provided sheltered anchorage along an otherwise exposed stretch of African coastline (centuries previously, the town, then known as Karikon Telichos, had been a trading post for Phoenician

*Carpets for sale*

traders). Later, at the end of the 19th century, the islands were used as a quarantine station for pilgrims returning from Mecca who might be importing plague, and more recently as a prison.

Today the islands have been turned into a bird sanctuary, especially for the Eleanora's falcon, and landings are prohibited.

Various operators such as Essa Evasion (tel: 0254-79 21 39, www.essa-evasion.com) runs daily boat trips around the islands, offering a close-up view of the decaying prison complex and the islands' abundant birdlife.

## THE MEDINA

Essaouira's main souk streets – Avenue de l'Istiqual and Avenue Sidi Mohammed Ben Abdallah – lie within the medina north of Place Moulay Hassan, with endless shops piled high with colourful souvenirs. Small archways and sections of wall subdivide the various sections of the medina, while walking southeast down Rue Mohammed el Qory brings you to the outer medina walls and the impressive Bab Marrakech, complete with huge circular bastion, the most impressive of the town's various gateways.

### Skala de la Ville

Turn left up Rue Derb Laâlouj from Avenue Sidi Mohammed to reach the town's second section of ramparts, the **Skala de la Ville ❹** (aka the Skala de la Kasbah), an imposing stretch of fortifications topped with dozens of European cannons, several of British manufacture, offered as gifts from merchants to the Sultan Mohammed Ben Abdullah.

Directly beneath the ramparts lies the small but fragrant carpenters' souk, crammed with little workshops in which craftsmen can be seen carving everything from boxes, bracelets, picture frames and chess sets through to tables and cabinets out of thuya and cedarwood. One of the finest woodworkers' souks in Morocco, it supplies shops and bazaars all over the country and abroad. To bring out the rich patina of thuya wood, the handicrafts are rubbed with cotton balls soaked in vegetable oil.

### Museums and galleries

From the ramparts return to Rue de la Skala and head along Rue Derb Laâlouj, which will take you past the **Sidi Mohammed Ben Abdallah Museum ❺** (Wed–Mon 9am–6pm; charge), a good place to find out about the town's Jewish and musical heritage as well as its arts and crafts.

There are also several good art galleries scattered about town. The **Galerie Damgaard ❻** (www.galeriedamgaard.com), on Avenue Oqba, has been exhibiting works by Essaouira's famous painters since 1988 and has a fantastic collection. At 4 Rue de Tetouan, Galerie la Kasbah (www.galerie-lakasbah.com) is set in an 18th-century riad; Galerie l'Arbre Bleu (www.facebook.com/Galerie

*Football on the beach*

LArbreBleu) is on 233 Rue Chbanate, while at 20 Rue Malek Ben el Morhal, local artist Youssef el Qaouatli (http://qaouatli.wordpress.com), shows and sells his work in his home. The Afalkay Art Gallery (9 Place Prince Moulay Hassan) is dedicated to the craft of wood-carving and has some beautiful thuya wood exhibits.

### THE BEACH

Late afternoon is a good time for a walk around the bay, so take a leisurely stroll along Boulevard Mohammed V, or, if you prefer, relax on the beach, where this route ends. On summer evenings the beach is floodlit, allowing football, volleyball and even swimming to continue late into the night. There are also several good restaurants along here, including the excellent **Chalet de la Plage**, see ❸, which is a good spot to watch the action over a seafood supper and a bottle of gris.

### Activities

The well-organised Club Mistral, (www.club-mistral.com) has surfboards, kite-surfs and windsurfs for rent. The Ranch de Diabet (tel: 0524-47 63 82, www.ranchdediabat.com) arranges rides (horse and camel) on the beach, into the surrounding countryside and to historic sites and marabouts. For those wanting more of a thrill, quad bikes can be hired from Quad Pro Isfaoun (tel: 0524-47 49 06), Sahara Quad (tel: 0673-44 95 41, www.saharaquad.net) and Palma Quad (tel: 0666-70 99 99, www.palmaquad.com).

### SOUTH OF ESSAOUIRA

Further along the coast, off the N1 rolling its way over the foothills of the High Atlas to Agadir, minor roads and tracks lead to what the Moroccans call *plages sauvages* (wild beaches), long stretches of white sand-duned beaches thickly fringed by prickly gorse and argan trees and disappearing into thin mists in the

---

## The Jewish legacy

For a small town, Essaouira has a substantial *mellah* (old Jewish quarter) and Jewish Cemetery (outside Bab Doukkala), reflecting the town's once-significant Jewish population. Jews were often middlemen for European and Arab merchants; in 1860, the British traveller and writer James Richards estimated that they comprised nearly one third of the town's 13–14,000-strong population. Among the prominent Jewish familes were the Disraelis, whose descendant Benjamin became one of Britain's most distinguished prime ministers. Very few Jews remain today, the majority having emigrated to Israel or Europe in the second half of the 20th century. A tiny synagogue still stands on Rue Ziry Ben Atiyah (off Rue Derb Laâlouj), but it is dilapidated and disused.

*Fishing boat*                    *Fisherman repairing a net*

distance. Surfers, who have been coming to Essaouira for years, frequent Cap Sim and Diabat.

### Sidi Kaouki

Sidi Kaouki, a beach just south of Essaouira, and dominated at its northern end by a spectacularly sited marabout shrine, offers an excellent and very accessible alternative to staying in Essaouira itself. It has become the focus for the more experienced surfing and windsurfing brigade, with a few places to stay, including the excellent Hotel Villa Soleil, with rooms overlooking the sea, and Windy Kaouki (www.windy-kaouki.com), where you can arrange watersports and horse-riding trips. Sidi Kaouki's superb sandy beach goes on for miles but it is prone to being very windy. The small tarmac road continues behind the beach along the coast, giving access to yet more stupendous beaches, some with rocky headlands offering reasonable windbreaks.

### Cap Tafelney

Cap Tafelney, surrounded by hills and sheltering a small community of picturesque fishing huts (some of which sell a frugal selection of sea-damp provisions), offers one of the coastline's longest undisturbed beaches for anyone willing to get away from the tiny tarmac access point on its northern end.

## Food and Drink

### ① PÂTISSERIE DRISS
23 Rue Hajjali; tel: 0524-47 57 93; 8am–10pm; €
The best spot for coffee and croissants in town, but also does tasty light meals later in the day.

### ② FISH STALLS
Between Place Moulay Hassan and the Harbour; €€
This enclave of little open-air fish restaurants decked out in blue-and-white awnings is an Essaouira institution, and a great place for lunch or dinner. Your choice of fish, from sardines to sea bass and lobster, is weighed and grilled while you pull up a chair at a communal table. Salad and a soft drink or water are normally included in the price. A word of warning, however: keep an eye on the scales when your fish is weighed and be prepared to query inflated prices; tourists are routinely ripped off.

### ③ CHALET DE LA PLAGE
Boulevard Mohammed V; tel: 0524-47 59 72; €€€
Large portions of good French and international food (emphasis on fish – the bouillabaisse is very good, as are the sea urchins when in season). It is possible just to drink at the bar and eat tapas. Very busy at weekends.

*Ourika Valley*

# THE OURIKA VALLEY

*When Marrakech gets too hot or hectic, locals and visitors alike head for the hills. The Ourika Valley, winding up between the mountains of the High Atlas, is one of the most accessible and popular such destinations, its slopes carpeted with wildflowers in spring, and offering a cool retreat from the city in the hot summer.*

**DISTANCE:** 126km (78 miles) round trip
**TIME:** A full day
**START/END:** Marrakech
**POINTS TO NOTE:** Despite the poor surface in the Ourika Valley, a non-4x4 vehicle is fine for this route. The tour is relatively easy, but many local operators run day trips into the valley. Hiring a private taxi for the day costs approximately 1,500DH. A grand taxi will cost around 450DH one way, and take up to six people.

Gazing south on a clear day from any rooftop in Marrakech you can't help but notice the magnificent horseshoe of mountains towering up from the flat plains surrounding the city. This is the High Atlas, home to North Africa's loftiest peak (Mount Toubkal) and traditional heartland of the country's mountain Berbers, a hardy race of mountain dwellers who still cling on to their traditional lifestyles in remote upland villages, as well as accounting for around half of the population of modern Marrakech.

The Ourika Valley, with its sheltered olive and walnut groves, where water flows year-round, offers a rewarding and convenient day trip into the Atlas, easily done by hire car or by private taxi. Be warned, however, that the valley is no longer a well-kept secret, and in summer *Marrakshis* head for the cool waters of the Ourika in their droves. The valley can be visited at any time of year. In winter the valley is cold and crisp, but rarely snow-covered, and in summer temperatures can be up to 15°C (22.5°F) cooler than in Marrakech.

## LEAVING MARRAKECH

Starting at the roundabout just the other side of the city wall from the landmark La Mamounia (see page 62), follow Boulevard El Yarmouk southward, keeping the ramparts on your left. In winter, and on clear days at other times of year, the panorama

of the Atlas Mountains in front of you will confirm that you are heading in the right direction.

As you leave the city you'll see the familiar picture-postcard shot of the 11th-century ramparts framed by date palms and the mountains. The route cuts across the flat and largely featureless Haouz Plain, on which wealthy Moroccans and foreigners have built lavish villas amid olive groves and fruit orchards. Such prosperity has also spawned numerous interior-design shops, garden centres and artisanal workshops, catering to the surge in demand created by the region's ever-increasing number of riads and villas.

## TNINE OURIKA

Follow the road for 33km (20 miles) until you arrive at the first major settlement and continue straight at the roundabout. Keep on for another 500m/yds, until you reach a left turn (signposted 'Jardin Nectarome') towards the village of **Tnine Ourika** ❶, a bustling regional centre set in olive groves below the foothills of the Atlas. Tnine means Monday in Arabic, and the town's Monday market is well worth a visit. Such souks have a hugely important socio-economic role to play in Berber society, although you are unlikely to find any really interesting bargains.

### Saffron Garden

Before you arrive at the village itself (a few hundred metres after the left turn), a sign will direct you to the **Saffron Garden** (Jardin du Safran; www.safran-ourika.com; daily 9am–6pm; charge). This privately owned saffron garden holds a small exhibition that demonstrates the various stages in the production of saffron, and all produce is sold on-site to visitors.

A visit to the garden is particularly worthwhile during the months of October or November, when women from the surrounding villages harvest the crop, which takes a year from planting before coming to fruition.

THE OURIKA VALLEY **73**

*Pottery workshop*

### Nectarome

Continuing into the village of Tnine, keep your eyes peeled for a sign off to the left to **Nectarome** (daily 9am–6pm; www.nectarome.com; charge), which is accessed by an 800m/yd dirt road (passable in a conventional vehicle) that starts opposite the police station *(Gendarmerie)*, just before the marketplace. This garden is a far more elaborate affair than the saffron garden and bills itself as an 'organic aromatic garden' dedicated to the study of essential oils and natural cosmetics. It is an interesting place to visit and has a shop (as well as an extensive online catalogue) selling the well-being products that are generated on site.

### Berber Ecomuseum

As you continue up the valley, around 4km (2.5 miles) beyond Tnine a small sign directs you up a dirt road to the village of Tafza. The village's old mud-brick kasbah has now been converted into the Ecomusée Berbère de l'Ourika (daily 9.30am–7pm; www.museeeberbere.com; charge). Exhibits include various Berber artefacts and some stunning historic photographs showing life in the mountains in decades past. Local guides run treks and tours offering rewarding insights into local life and culture in the valley.

### OURIKA VALLEY

As you continue southwards along the valley, the Ourika River shortly comes into view, cutting its way through the first of the many olive-tree plantations that characterise the **Ourika Valley** ❷ (Vallée de l'Ourika). Traditional adobe villages can still be seen on the far side of the river, although the results of modern tourism (and subsequent influxes of cash) can be seen in the more modern concrete buildings lining the road itself. Assorted carpet bazaars have also sprung up along the road, although carpet-making isn't native to the valley, which is best known for its pottery. Most of the shops have workshops and kilns that you can visit if you are interested, although you'll be expected to make a small purchase if you visit.

If you need some lunch while driving along the valley road, there are plenty of Berber restaurants at which to stop (see page 76).

### Mountain activities

As you head on from the villages of the lower Ourika, the road winds its way gradually up the increasingly steep-sided valley. At the 43km (26-mile) mark you'll pass a right turn to **Oukaimiden**, which, at 2,700m (8,858ft) above sea level, is North Africa's highest ski station. From the junction the road climbs steeply for around 30km (20 miles) up to the resort, which boasts basic accommodation, two ski lifts and equipment-hire shops. The season is short (December to February) but snow can never be guaranteed, even in win-

*Fresh mint for sale*

ter. Facilities are rudimentary, and there are only a couple of slopes, but the low-key informality of Oukaimiden is part of the charm. You can hire equipment and arrange lessons with the enterprising locals, and there are also a couple of hotels including the characterful Chez Ju-Ju inn (tel: 0524-31 90 05; www.hotelchezjuju.com). Although it can get busy at weekends, when wealthy Marrakshis descend en masse, on weekdays the resort is virtually empty. During the summer months the area offers plenty of interesting and scenic hiking possibilities.

### Along the Ourika Road

A few hundred metres after the Oukaimiden turn-off, the village of **Aghbalou** has a small Thursday souk (signposted down a steep track off to the left). Onward from here there are a number of busy villages offering riverside eating facilities popular with Moroccan day-trippers. It is not until the approach to Setti Fatma, though, that the full drama of the High Atlas begins to unfold.

### SETTI FATMA

**Setti Fatma ❸**, a small but lively trail-head village, is the end of the line for non-4x4 vehicles. Located at the end of the tarmac road, 60km (37 miles) from Marrakech, the village is hemmed in by towering limestone cliffs. The main attraction is the series of seven water-falls on the far side of the river, the first

## Berber architecture

The villages that flank the eastern side of the Ourika Valley, and many of the small settlements that line the route up to Oukaimiden, contain excellent examples of Berber High Atlas vernacular, which, in this region, dates back centuries. The architecture is simple and at times austere; few changes have been made to building materials or practices over the years.

Here, construction is all about making use of raw materials that are found in the region, where earth, straw, sand and stone are blended to build dwellings that are both environmentally sound and sit in harmony with their surroundings. Some villagers choose to build their houses with adobe bricks, a strong and resilient mud brick made with a wooden framework and left to dry prior to being laid; others favour *pisé*, a similar mix of earth, straw and sand compressed in between rows of wooden shuttering and left to dry. Roofs are rarely pitched, and are constructed of eucalyptus beams on to which plastic sheeting (for water-proofing) is laid, before a final coat of mud is applied.

The thermal properties of earth houses in the extreme climate of Morocco are unrivalled by most modern building materials, but, as the population grows in wealth, it is expected that traditional building methods will be used less.

*A Setti Fatma waterfall*

of which is reached after an easy climb through the rocks and trees. In the summer this is a popular spot for tourists and Marrakchis alike, with swimming in a deep, icy rock pool, while above, wild monkeys stalk the craggy heights and shower walnuts on the unwary.

### Hiking options

Setti Fatma is the staging post for some exciting treks into the heart of

the High Atlas. A two-day hike takes you to Oukaimiden (see page 74), and three days of trekking takes you to Imlil (see page 80), at the foot of Mount Toubkal, the highest mountain in North Africa.

On arrival in Setti Fatma you may be accosted by locals wishing to take you to the waterfalls above the village or to local bazaars. Choosing an official guide (most of whom speak English) from Imlil's Bureau des Guides (tel: 0524-48 56 26), the centre for registered guides in the region, is a good way to buy some peace and quiet.

You can do treks of various lengths. For the hikes in the Atlas or up to the waterfalls, you will need to wear solid walking shoes that are suitable for mountainous and rocky terrain. For those hikers seeking a more gentle stroll, continue through the village and follow the river through a U-shaped valley lined with village houses. The scenery here is fabulous.

Of all the many places to eat in the village – most of them serving traditional local food – one of the best is **La Perle d'Ourika** (see box).

### RETURN TO MARRAKECH

After time to enjoy your surroundings, retrace your path back to Marrakech for an early evening aperitif in your hotel. The journey back, without stops to refuel or shop, takes about an hour and a half.

---

### Food and Drink

Numerous restaurants line the Ourika Valley road, all specialising in Berber home cooking. This plays on the strengths of ingredients available in the immediate vicinity, with lamb or beef stews (tajines) made with locally grown (mainly root) vegetables the preferred main dish, and couscous on Fridays. Corn soups (dshisha), chickpea soup (harira) and bean stews (lubia) are also a popular way to ward off the winter chill of the mountains.

Setti Fatma teems with restaurants serving Berber specialities. Try **La Perle d'Ourika** (tel: 061-567239; www.laperle dourika.com), run by the lovely Ammaria. Otherwise there is a cluster alongside the river. As a rule, opt for the busier restaurants (they will have a faster turnover of food), particularly those that seem popular with locals, or check at the Bureau des Guides as to which of the many restaurants is currently worth seeking out.

*Kasbah du Toubkal*

# IMLIL AND MOUNT TOUBKAL

*Mountain lovers and hikers should head for Imlil, a Berber village in the heart of the Toubkal National Park, amid shady walnut groves at the foot of North Africa's highest peak, with unspoilt scenery and hikes to suit all levels.*

**DISTANCE:** 190km (118 miles) round trip
**TIME:** Possible as a long day trip, but better with a night in Imlil
**START/END:** Marrakech
**POINTS TO NOTE:** This excursion can be undertaken in a non-4x4 rental vehicle, and all of the route is along tarmac roads. Without a hire car the trip can be undertaken in a private taxi, (around 1,500DH for the day). A grand taxi will cost 400DH one way, and take up to six people. Should you wish to go hiking in Toubkal National Park, the Bureau des Guides in Imlil can organise multi-day, fully catered, mule-supported treks. These are best booked at least a few days in advance. The best time of year to hike in the region is between April and November, when high passes are not blocked by heavy snowfalls.

Less developed than the neighbouring Ourika Valley, the Mizane Valley links the Berber settlements of Asni and Imlil, and offers an enthralling glimpse of life in the High Atlas Mountains. A land where cloaked figures shuffle into mountainside mosques, womenfolk harvest crops in immaculately terraced fields, and the pace of life slows to a virtual standstill.

At the head of the valley, the popular trailhead village of Imlil generates an atmosphere all of its own and makes an excellent base or starting point for walks into the surrounding mountains. A rewarding two-day hike takes you up to the summit of the country's highest peak, while there are also other rewarding but less strenuous trekking possibilities, most notably walks in the untouched Tacheddirt Valley, across the Tamatert Pass from Imlil.

If you plan to stay the night in the Toubkal National Park, reserve accommodation in advance, particularly in spring and autumn, when the Imlil area gets very busy.

The Marigha/Ouirgane area boasts several good places to stay, including the Provençal-style La Bergerie (see page 108), the elegant Domaine de la Roseraie (see page 108) and the traditional Berber lodge Dar Tassa (tel:

*Mizane Valley*

0524-48 43 12; www.dartassa.co.uk). Note also that you'll need to bring your own sleeping bag if you're planning to hike up Mount Toubkal (see page 80).

## LEAVING MARRAKECH

Setting off from the roundabout alongside the city wall at La Mamounia hotel, head south, keeping the ramparts on your left. Ignore the first right turn (signposted 'aéroport') and take the second right turn a couple of hundred metres further on. This is the R203 (signposted 'Taroudant'), a road that eventually runs into the infamous Tizi-n-Test (see page 95), one of the highest and most precipitous passes in North Africa. Keep your speed below 60kph (37mph) along this stretch of road (a well-known police speed-trap) and continue until you reach a fork in the road after a further 5km (3 miles) or so.

Take the left fork and remain on this rather nondescript route until you arrive in the village of **Tahanaoute**, an important regional centre set in an immense olive grove. Continue straight on at the mini roundabout and follow the road, which, after a few kilometres, begins to climb into the foothills of the High Atlas.

## ASNI

The first village you arrive at, some 47km (29 miles) from Marrakech, is **Asni ❶** (see page 93), which has an important Saturday souk. Every week the market here attracts from far and wide villagers who descend on the village to trade goods, do business and discuss the week's events over a glass of impossibly sweet mint tea.

There's little to see or do in Asni but it makes a convenient place to stop for a tea or coffee break en route, although on market days you're likely to be swamped by crowds of visiting locals.

## MARIGHA

Just beyond Asni, a left turn (signposted 'Imlil') takes you up the Mizane Valley along a scenic route to Imlil and the gateway to the Toubkal National Park. Note this turn-off but continue along the same (Tizi-n-Test) route that snakes its way down a valley of green oak and juniper bushes to the village of **Marigha ❷**, after a further 10km (6 miles).

In the village, which appears from the road to be little more than a few houses, turn right at the crossroads (signposted 'Amizmiz') and then turn right into the car park of **L'Oliveraie de Marigha**, see ❶, where you can have some lunch among attractive surroundings and, if you fancy it, a spot of relaxation by the pool.

## MIZANE VALLEY

After lunch head back up the winding road towards Asni and take the Imlil turn-off (on your right). The 17km (10-mile) road passes through the **Mizane**

*The main street in Imlil*

**Valley** (Vallée de Mizane), where a thin strip of cultivation on the valley floor is framed by stark peaks. Traditional mud villages cling to the hillsides here. The Mizane river flows year-round and irrigates villagers' vegetable patches and groves of walnut and almond trees.

## Kasbah Tamadot

After a few kilometres you will pass **Kasbah Tamadot** (see page 109), the British entrepreneur Richard Branson's hotel retreat, a rambling kasbah-style building set in lavish gardens overlooking the valley. It's luxurious, with prices to match.

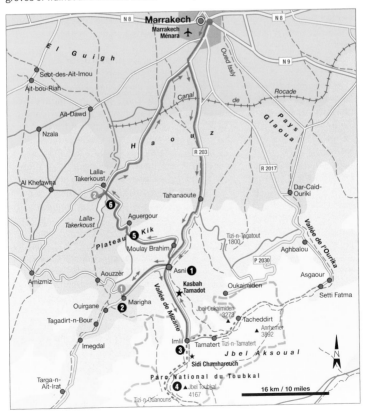

*The slopes of Mount Toubkal*

## IMLIL

Arriving in **Imlil** ❸, look out for a sign welcoming you to the **Toubkal National Park** (Parc National du Toubkal), one of the main reasons for visiting this bustling High Atlas village. Continue into the village, where you'll see a parking area to the left after a couple of hundred metres (next to the Bureau des Guides). Here you can leave your car with the parking attendant for 10DH or so.

Imlil is the High Atlas's most commercial village, but compensates with its extraordinary surrounding scenery. Here, Moroccan day-trippers congregate along the river banks and hikers start and finish the trek up Mount Toubkal, the highest mountain in Africa to the north of the equator.

### Kasbah du Toubkal

In the village walk up the main street (left out of the car park), then take the first right (after a couple of hundred metres), along a road lined with souvenir shops. From here follow signs along a steep (and moderately strenuous) winding track shaded by walnut trees up to the **Kasbah du Toubkal** hotel (http://www.kasbahdutoubkal.com), in a spectacular location overlooking the valley. The hotel, which doubled as a Tibetan temple in Martin Scorsese's film *Kundun*, has a range of luxurious rooms (advance booking essential), a unique location and impressive

responsible-tourism credentials. The 15- to 20-minute walk up to the site is worth the effort, whether you go inside the Kasbah or not.

### Guide services

Return to Imlil and head back to the car park. The **Bureau des Guides** (tel: 0524-48 56 26; on the left as you face the river) can provide maps of the area, plus assistance and advice regarding local treks. Guides (and mules to carry bags) are usually available at short notice, meaning that you can generally set up a hike (including the ascent of Mount Toubkal) for the following day if that's what you what.

### Climbing Toubkal

From Imlil it takes two days to reach the summit of **Mount Toubkal** ❹ (Jbel Toubkal), which, at 4,167m (13,671ft) above sea level, is North Africa's highest mountain. The well-trodden path south from Imlil, at 1,500m (4,920ft), up to the roof of North Africa, is a remorseless hike, broken by an overnight stop at the CAF (Club Alpin Français) refuge at some 3,200m (10,500ft).

The Toubkal National Park is subject to rapid changes in climatic conditions, so make sure that you pack appropriate clothing. Waterproof and windproof jackets are essential, even in summer, as are good walking boots. Don't attempt the ascent between late November and June unless you have snow-climbing experience. Crampons

*Mules can be hired*        *Kasbah du Toubkal dining room*

can be hired in Imlil, although they're often substandard and it's better to bring your own. Although certified local mountain guides (ask to see their official ID cards) will have received training in snow climbing, you are recommended to book winter ascents through a bonafide tour operator.

The first day's walk is a five- to six-hour haul up from Imlil, via the holy shrine *(marabout)* of **Sidi Chamharouch**, to the well-equipped but rather bleak CAF refuge. Hot meals are served here, and dormitory accommodation provided (bring your own sleeping bag). There's also a rocky camping area downstream from the refuge for those equipped with tents.

The ascent follows a path leading eastwards from the refuge and includes some steep sections towards the top of the climb. While the hike doesn't involve any rock climbing, it's strenuous and steep enough to deter those who are not accustomed to mountain trekking. To tackle the climb, try to set off early, as clouds often close in on the summit after midday. The walk up from the refuge takes approximately three hours; fit walkers can then return to Imlil on the same day, rather than stay another night in the uninspiring refuge.

On a clear day the views from the top of Toubkal, out towards the northern fringes of the Sahara Desert, are magnificent, making the peak a worthwhile challenge.

### Tamatert Pass and Tacheddirt

The best overnight accommodation option around Imlil is the lovely **Douar Samra** (tel: 0524-48 40 34; www.douar-samra.com), a stylish Berber guesthouse in the hamlet of **Tamatert**, 3km (2 miles) east of Imlil. It offers amazing views and excellent Moroccan home-cooking.

Douar Samra is set about halfway up the **Tamatert Pass**, over which lies the village of **Tacheddirt**, said to be the highest of its size in the High Atlas. Despite its remoteness the village is changing fast, with growing numbers of visitors venturing out here along the (now surfaced) road through the village between Imlil and Oukaimiden.

Set in a wide rolling valley, Tacheddirt and its neighbouring villages are a delight, and the valley offers rewarding walking. Day hikes with an English-speaking guide can be arranged from Douar Samra up the pass. These will take you through glorious villages that are still isolated enough to preserve a fiercely traditional way of life.

### OVER THE KIK PLATEAU

After spending a night or two in the mountains, head back on the road to Asni. Turn left at the T-junction in Asni taking the road towards Tahanaoute and Marrakech.

Shortly after the avenue of eucalyptus trees at the exit to the village, take the left turn that leads along a tarmac road up to **Moulay Brahim**, a moun-

*Paragliding over Kik Plateau*

tain-top village that attracts pilgrims and day-trippers from Marrakech, although there's little here to interest foreign visitors.

Continue to the **Kik Plateau** ❺, a rolling expanse of wheat fields (in season) punctuated by scenic hamlets and overlooked by some of the highest peaks in the Atlas range.

The plateau loses some of its appeal in the dry summer and early autumn months, but during late winter and throughout spring it is one of the most magical places in the High Atlas, with breathtaking views down towards Lalla-Takerkoust and the town of Amizmiz, and fields of poppies framed by dramatic snow-capped mountains.

It's possible to hike here or, if you have a 4x4 vehicle, explore the off-road pistes that traverse the area. In spring, it's nice to take a picnic with you when you're exploring the plateau. Most hotels can prepare one picnic for you (ask the night before).

### LALLA-TAKERKOUST

Follow the tarmac road across the plateau and then down on to the Haouz Plain, where you will find the lake of **Lalla-Takerkoust** ❻. This barrage is the source of most of Marrakech's water, which is carried down to the city along man-made canals.

The lake is a pleasant enough spot for a stroll, and the French-owned hotel/restaurant **Relais du Lac**, see ❷, on the far shore, is a good choice for lunch with a view.

### RETURN TO MARRAKECH

From the restaurant, head back around the lake and turn right on to the main road, from where it is a 33km (20-mile) drive back to Marrakech.

---

## Food and Drink

### ❶ L'OLIVERAIE DE MARIGHA

Marigha, Route d'Amizmiz par Asni; tel: 0524-48 42 81; www.oliveraie-de-marigha.com; noon–3pm & 7–9pm; €€

Set in olive groves with excellent views, this Provençal-style garden restaurant serves light lunches such as salads and brochettes and offers diners use of its excellent swimming pool (non-diners 150DH). Alcohol served.

### ❷ RELAIS DU LAC

Route du Lac, Route d'Amizmiz, Lalla-Takerkoust; tel: 0524-48 49 43; www.relaisdulacmarrakech.com; daily, all day; €€

Pleasant lakeside restaurant with superb views over the lake of Lalla-Takerkoust and out to the High Atlas foothills. Food includes simple Moroccan staples and French dishes such as steak and brochettes. Indoor and outdoor dining available.

*Ait-Benhaddou*

# TIZI-N-TICHKA TO ZAGORA

*South of the High Atlas, the landscape changes dramatically, turning to desert as it approaches the fringes of the vast Saharan sands, its red-rock mountains and arid valleys dotted with crumbling mudbrick kasbahs, sprawling oases and rolling dunes.*

**DISTANCE:** 850km (528 miles) round trip
**TIME:** Best as a 3- or 4-day trip
**START/END:** Marrakech
**POINTS TO NOTE:** This excursion can be undertaken in a rental vehicle, and, apart from a short sandy section to the dunes of Tinfou and a rough jeep-road to Oasis Fint, all of the route is surfaced. While bus services exist between Marrakech and Ouarzazate, and Ouarzazate and Zagora, this route is hard to accomplish this way as there are many stops en route.

The sweeping plains and mountain ranges south of Tizi-n-Tichka (Tichka Pass) have some of Morocco's most captivating sights. The spectacular mudbrick village of Ait-Benhaddou and the Draa Valley are just two of the many highlights along the road from the High Atlas Mountains to the Sahara Desert, and, for those with time and a hire car, the road-trip from Marrakech to Zagora is one of Morocco's most memorable trips. The best times to travel around the area are spring and autumn. The blistering summer months (July–Sept) are best avoided, given the high temperatures at that time of year.

## LEAVING MARRAKECH

From the bus station at Bab Doukkala drive out of the city on the Fez road, heading east with the city wall on your right. This road takes you for a kilometre around the perimeter of the medina, until you reach a roundabout with the Bab el Khemis market on your right.

From here, continue straight on for 7km (4 miles), then turn right at the major roundabout onto the N9, which climbs over the Atlas Mountains before dropping down to the city of Ouarzazate.

### Across the Haouz Plain

As with all routes out of the city, the road traverses the fertile and prosperous **Haouz Plain**, dotted with olive groves and citrus orchards, as well as fancy villa complexes belonging to wealthy Moroccans and expats.

*The Tichka Pass*

## THE ATLAS FOOTHILLS

Continuing along this road you'll pass the market town of **Ait-Ourir ❶**, 36km (22 miles) from Marrakech, which has an interesting Berber Tuesday souk on the left side of the main road.

Past Ait-Ourir, the landscape begins to change, as the road starts climbing into the foothills of the High Atlas. After the fertile **Zat Valley** (Vallée du Zat, on your right), olive trees give way to pines, juniper and green oak, as the road climbs into the mountains. If you want a break there are a number of cafés offering panoramic mountain views from their terraces.

### Taddert

Carry on as far as **Taddert ❷**, a bustling one-street village some 99km (61 miles) from Marrakech at the foot of the winding Tichka Pass. You may not fancy the rows of meat hanging in the roadside butchers' shops (choose your cut and then select a restaurant to barbeque it for you), but as it's the last truck stop before the Pass it's a good place to buy snacks or stop for refreshments.

## TIZI-N-TICHKA

Past Taddert, the road snakes its way up a series of breathtaking switchbacks before a flatter section leads you to the top of the **Tizi-n-Tichka Pass ❸**, 2,260m (7,414ft) above sea level. The road over the top is one of North Africa's highest paved roads, announced by souvenir shops and a café, where you can expect the hardsell treatment should you decide to stop. Be aware also of the carpet-sell-

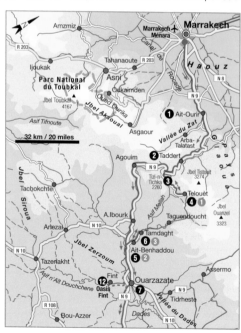

*Sign marking the altitude*

*Turn–off to Telouèt*

ing scam on the road just south of the Tichka Pass. Don't stop for anyone requesting help with a supposedly broken-down vehicle, since fake breakdowns of this nature are a ruse for getting into tourists' cars to take them to carpet shops.

## TELOUÈT

A few kilometres over the top of the Tichka Pass you'll reach a left turn signed to Telouèt. Turn down this poorly surfaced tarmac road and continue for 20km (12 miles) to reach the village of **Telouèt** ❹ itself, home to one of Morocco's most celebrated *kasbahs* (walled fortresses). To reach it, continue through the village and then turn right immediately beyond the elaborately stone-clad **Auberge Telouèt**, see ❶. This takes you into the kasbah complex, where you can park.

### The kasbah

The Telouèt kasbah was built over four centuries (from the 17th to 20th) but gained particular notoriety as the residence of Thami el Glaoui, a Berber tribal chief, ex-governor of Marrakech and supporter of the French during the protectorate period. After Morocco was granted independence in 1956, the Glaoui family was left disgraced and dispossessed, and Thami el Glaoui died of natural causes soon after.

Since then, the kasbah has remained uninhabited and these days

is a crumbling, elegant ruin, a shadow of its once-spectacular self. For a small fee (15DH or so, payable to the custodian on the door) you can have a look round the most recently built quarter of the kasbah. The older section of the kasbah (to the right as you drive down the access road) can be viewed from the rooftop, but, as you will see, is little more than a pile of crumbling earth inhabited by a family of storks.

A spectacular piste (a continuation of the tarmac road through Telouèt) runs from Telouèt to Ait-Benhaddou, heading south through the scenic Ounila Valley. It's rough, however, and should only be tackled in a 4x4 vehicle and by those with experience of off-road driving.

For lunch, try the restaurants serving simple tajines around the central square.

## INTO THE SOUTH

After lunch, drive back to the N9 highway and turn left, continuing towards Ouarzazate. The well-maintained road winds through a few roadside villages before straightening out as it leaves the mountains. Check the roadside distance markers, as you'll need to turn left 23km (14 miles) before Ouarzazate.

The left turn, about 65km (40 miles) from the point where you rejoined the N9, is signposted 'Tamdaght' and 'Ait-Benhaddou' and is relatively easy to spot. Heading north along this road you'll have the whole majestic panorama of the High Atlas in front of you as

*Building in Ait–Benhaddou*

you drive through a desolate landscape dotted with the occasional date palm. After 9km (5 miles) you'll arrive at a village where you'll see a parking area off to your right. Leave your car here and walk down a cobbled alleyway (running the gauntlet of souvenir shops) and then across a small wooden bridge to reach the dramatic *ksar* (fortified village) of Ait-Benhaddou.

## Local film industry

Since Orson Welles' 1952 classic, *Othello*, was filmed in Essaouira, Morocco has attracted foreign film-makers seduced by the country's clear light and amazing landscapes. Focus has now shifted to the kasbahs and deserts of the south: *Lawrence of Arabia* and *Gladiator* are just two in a long line of epics filmed around Ouarzazate, the home of Moroccan cinema. Proximity to Europe, an excellent infrastructure, minimal bureaucracy and the availability of cheap labour are further incentives for film companies.

For an intriguing taste of Ouarzazate's cinematic credentials, pay a visit to the rambling Atlas Studios a few kilometres west of town along the main road (Oct–Feb 8.15am–5.15pm, Mar–Sept until 6.45pm; charge; www.studiosatlas.com), home to an extraordinary collection of huge, slightly battered-looking constructions from former shoots, including impressive film-sets used in movies ranging from *Astérix and Obélix* to *Gladiator*.

## AIT-BENHADDOU

The fortified village of **Ait-Benhaddou** ❺ is as magnificent an example of kasbah architecture as you will find in Morocco – or anywhere else, for that matter. A great mass of mud-brick houses rising above the rocky riverbed (dry for much of the year), Ait-Benhaddou is one of southern Morocco's most extraordinary sights, so picture-perfect and dramatically stage-managed that it looks almost like some kind of supersized film set. Not surprisingly, the village has proved a major hit with cinema directors, featuring in numerous Hollywood epics such as *Lawrence of Arabia*, *The Sheltering Sky* and *Gladiator*.

Now designated a Unesco World Heritage Site, the earliest buildings here date back to the 11th century, built around a warren of tiny streets and even tinier alleyways

The village is still inhabited by a handful of families, some of whom may offer to show you around their houses for a small fee (10–15DH or so).

There are numerous cafés, restaurants and inns in the newer part of town, near the car park. A good choice is **Dar Mouna**, see ❷.

## TAMDAGHT

Continue north in the same direction for a further 6km (4 miles) along the road from Ait Benhaddou. A spectacu-

*Ait-Benhaddou fortifications*

*Atlas Studios, Ouarzazate*

lar ruined kasbah overlooking a valley of almond trees announces your arrival at **Tamdaght** ❻, another village on a once-important trade route connecting Marrakech with the Draa Valley and Sahara Desert.

Just before the end of the tarmac road, with the kasbah on your left, is a short section of piste that takes you into the *ksar*. Then follow the signs to **Kasbah Ellouze**, see ❸, a stylish French-run guesthouse. This comfortable 10-bedroom *maison d'hôte* comes as quite a surprise, lost among the crumbling ruins of Morocco's turbulent past, and makes an excellent and uncommercial place to stay for the night, and with good food too.

## OUARZAZATE

Starting out on day two, head back to the Marrakech–Ouarzazate road and turn left. A further 23km (14 miles) brings you to **Ouarzazate** ❼, a rather nondescript administrative centre that grew up as a base of the French Foreign Legion. The town is something of a crossroads between Marrakech to the north, the Draa Valley (see page 87) to the south, the Dades and Todra gorges to the east and Taroudant (see page 96) and Agadir (see page 97) to the west. Notice on your way into town a couple of giant foreign-owned film studios, evidence of the importance the film industry to the local economy (see page 86).

### Kasbah Taourirt

In the town itself, the only attraction of any real note is the **Kasbah Taourirt** (on the main road at the far end of town; no tel.; daily 8am–6pm; charge), a huge complex, the size of a small town, originally built by the Glaoui dynasty for their local chiefs, retainers and myriad servants. Much of the kasbah has fallen into ruin, although small sections have now been patched up with Unesco assistance, including the original residence of the Glaoui rulers, complete with traces of its lavish decoration, surrounded by a beautiful little labyrinth of mudbrick houses and twisting alleyways, hemmed in behind high walls.

## DRAA VALLEY

Starting at the kasbah, drive back into the centre of town, and turn left at a set of traffic lights just before the shops, with the **tourist office** on your left. This route takes you across the river on what is effectively a continuation of the N9 from Marrakech.

Once you have crossed to the south side of the river, bear left along the same road and leaving the urban sprawl of Ouarzazate behind. The road to Agdz leads through an undulating moonscape, winding its way up bare volcanic slopes before eventually dropping down into the **Draa Valley** (Vallée du Draa) – a swathe of intensive cultivation in an otherwise barren land.

*Agdz's weekly market*

The Draa river, although dry for much of its course, is the country's longest, and the section of the valley between Ouarzazate and Zagora is a major date-producing region, home to an estimated eight million date palms. Only the female date palms bear fruit, with each tree producing about 80kg (176lb) of dates. The date harvest is in November, when locals shin up the trees, cut down the dates and sun-dry them on woven mats.

On your way down the Draa Valley, look out on your left for signs marked '*Circuit de la Palmeraie*', a network of roads leading into the heart of the Draa's magnificent palm plantations.

### Agdz

The first riverside settlement is **Agdz** ❶, named, some say, after the letters emblazoned on the side of a plane that crashed in the valley in the early 1900s. On arrival, pass through the arch and, at the point where the main road dog-legs right, turn left down a side street. Continue for a few hundred metres along this road, keeping a lookout for a right-turn signed 'Dar Qamar'.

Follow the narrow dirt road between two mud walls into the car park of the idyllic French-owned **Dar Qamar**, see ❹, buried deep in the Agdz kasbah. You can have lunch here (book ahead), while it also makes a memorable place for an overnight stay (see page 109).

### Kasbah Tamnougalte

After lunch, head back to the Ouarzazate–Zagora road and then turn left towards Zagora. After 5km (3 miles), at a right-hand bend in the road, you will see a piste that crosses one of the channels of the Draa river. Turn left here and follow the unpaved road (rough in places but passable in a conventional car), skirting an impressive kasbah perched upon a hill to your left.

Continue until you reach an easy-to-miss right turn after another 500m/yds and follow this track through an arch-way into a small parking area. To your right you will see the entrance to **Kasbah Tamnougalte** ❾ (daily 9am–6pm; charge). Here you can pay an English-speaking guide to show you around this well-preserved 16th-century house that was formerly the residence of the *Caïd* (district administrator) of the region. He lived here with his harem, and the house is now something of a museum piece.

To the left of the kasbah, the **Chez Yacob** guesthouse (tel: 0524-84 33 94; www.lavalleedudraa.com) occupies another restored kasbah preserving many of its original features – a nice place for a coffee or a meal on its terrace restaurant.

### Towards Zagora

Return to the main road and turn left along the main road for the final 90km (55 miles) to Zagora, along one of the most fascinating routes in Morocco.

*Dates for sale in Agdz*

*Draa Valley*

The villages of the Draa feel significantly more African than their counterparts in the High Atlas, reflecting the fact that the Draa served as a major trade route from sub-Saharan Africa during the 16th and 17th centuries.

As you drive further south you will also start to notice the physical impact of the Sahara Desert on the landscape, as acacia and tamarind trees dominate an increasingly desertified terrain. To the east, the anvil-shaped **Mount Kissane** (Jbel Kissane) marks the gateway to the magnificent **Mount Saghro (Jbel Saghro)**, a winter trekking paradise accessed from the attractive adobe village of **N'kob**, a turn-off some 29km (18 miles) south of Agdz. As the towering metropolises of mud and *palmeraies* (palm groves) multiply on either side of the road, the Sahara begins to make its presence increasingly felt, costumes change, and the colourfully clad women of the mountains are replaced by black-swathed and much darker-skinned people, originating from Mali and Mauritania. As the road approaches Zagora, the changes are ever more noticeable, the enclosed villages more densely packed, and reed-built palisades check the growing quantities of drifting sand.

## ZAGORA AND TINFOU

The town of **Zagora** ⑩ is the main market of the south of the country. With its drab breeze-block architecture, it comes as a bit of a disappointment after the journey, although the remains of an 11th-century Almoravid fortress clinging to the side of

*Palms in the Draa Valley*

Mount Zagora, on the south side of the river, offer a reminder of the town's antiquity.

Zagora once sat at a major confluence of trade routes. For centuries, Arabs, Berbers, Jews, Tuareg and Sahrawi people have coexited peacefully in this region, with the Jews being of particular importance in paving the way for trade all over the south.

Trans-Saharan caravans from the south would break their journey here before continuing east and north – as a much-photographed signpost pointing towards Timbuktu (a mere 52 days march by camel) suggests.

Otherwise, there's not a great deal to see in Zagora, but for sand-dune enthusiasts, daylight hours permitting, you can continue through the town (on the road to M'hamid) towards the dunes of **Tinfou** ⓫, 28km (17 miles) southeast of Zagora. Here you'll find a cluster of sand dunes on a wide, sweeping plain flanked by the **Jbel Tadrart** mountain range. The dunes (signposted left from the main road) are now rather touristy, with plenty of locals touting camel rides if you fancy a brief tour atop a dromedary around the dunes.

The true dunes of the Sahara begin approximately 70km (43 miles) south in **M'hamid**, at the end of the tarmac road. A trip to M'hamid is beyond the scope of this itinerary, but you might consider extending your trip to incorporate a desert safari starting from there, allowing at least an extra two days.

### Accommodation options

After watching the sunset from the Tinfou dunes, drive back to Zagora and check into your hotel. The **Fibule du Draa** (tel: 0524-84 73 18) is an efficient three-star hotel on the southeast side of the river, with a restaurant and an appealing pool, see ❺. For a true flavour of the Moroccan south, however, try **Dar Raha** (tel: 0524-84 69 93; www.darraha.com) in **Amezrou** village, 1km (0.6 miles) south of Zagora, a sober but stylish adobe house with simple, reasonably priced rooms and delicious home-cooking. The guesthouse is run by French anthropologist, Antoine Bouillon, who will be delighted to show you round the historic village and explain his work to increase awareness of the culture of the Draa.

### RETURN VIA OUARZAZATE

The 368km (228-mile) journey back to Marrakech is possible in a (very long) day, but it is better to break the journey in Ouarzazate.

On the edge of the city, just before you reach the first houses, look for a signpost to the *maison d'hôte* **Dar Daïf** (see page 109) and then follow the signs to this attractive guest house overlooked by the scenic ruins of the Stork's Kasbah (Kasbah de la Cigogne).

### Oasis Fint

Drive back the following morning to the main road and turn left at the first

*River Draa in the dry season*

junction (rather than crossing the river to go into the centre of the city). This route is effectively a bypass that rejoins the Ouarzazate–Marrakech road after a few kilometres. For those who have the time, a left turn off this route (sign-posted 'Fint') takes you along a rocky unpaved road to the **Oasis Fint** ⓬, one of the most picturesque in southern Morocco and a veritable paradise for photographers.

From here, return to the main road and continue back over the Tizi-n-Tichka Pass and down to Marrakech.

---

## Food and Drink

**❶ AUBERGE TELOUÈT**
Entrance to Kasbah Telouèt; tel: 0524-89 07 17; daily lunch and dinner; €
A good option for a set lunch of tajine or couscous under a camel-hair tent overlooking the Telouèt Kasbah.
Can be crowded with day-trippers and 4x4 parties.

**❷ DAR MOUNA**
Ksar Ait-Benhaddou; tel: 0528-84 30 54; www.darmouna.com; daily lunch and dinner; €€
As impressive views go, Dar Mouna's panorama of Ait-Benhaddou is hard to beat. This adobe guesthouse serves reliably high-quality Moroccan cuisine on the terrace, or, in the evening, in the rustic dining room. Set menu only.

**❸ KASBAH ELLOUZE**
Kasbah Tamdaght, Tamdaght; tel: 0524-89 04 59; www.kasbah ellouze.com; daily, non-guests for dinner only; €€
Run by French chef Michel Guillen, Kasbah Ellouze is a stylish converted kasbah guesthouse that serves a three-course Moroccan-style set menu. Non-guests must reserve in advance.

**❹ DAR QAMAR**
Kasbah d'Agdz, Agdz; tel: 0524-84 37 84; www.locsudmaroc.com; daily lunch and dinner; €€
Dar Qamar, an oasis of comfort in the crumbling Agdz kasbah, is a guesthouse that serves meals (lunch or dinner) by advance booking. The food served is generally Moroccan (the obligatory tajine or couscous), and part of a set menu that is included for guests on half-board.

**❺ FIBULE DU DRAA**
Route de M'hamid, just over the bridge in Amezrou; tel: 0524-84 73 18; daily lunch and dinner; €€
At this family-run hotel-restaurant, diners sit on low chairs in a vast Moroccan 'salon' and choose from a long list of well-prepared national favourites such as minced beef and egg tajine (*kefta aux oeufs*) and couscous served with lamb and sultanas.

*View from the Tizi-n-Test*

# TIZI-N-TEST TO TAROUDANT

*For a smaller, mellower version of Marrakech, head over the dramatic pass of Tizi-n-Test to Taroudant, an attractive walled city in the fertile Souss Valley. Along the way is one of Morocco's most historic mosques and also, rather more surprisingly, one of Africa's most exclusive hotel hideaways.*

**DISTANCE:** 446km (280 miles) returning via Tizi-n-Test; 765km (475 miles) via Agadir

**TIME:** 2–3 days

**START/END:** Marrakech

**POINTS TO NOTE:** The Tizi-n-Test from Marrakech to Taroudant is a paved road, perfectly manageable in a basic hire vehicle. Private and collective taxis also operate along this route, as do public bus services, but really to take advantage of the journey and its associated stops en route you are recommended to hire a car. If you wish to visit the Agoundis Valley, it is necessary to hire a 4x4 vehicle.

Of all the mountain passes in Morocco, Tizi-n-Test is arguably the most dramatic. The pass marks the watershed between the more fertile northern slopes of the High Atlas and the largely barren south, and the dizzying route offers a variety of landscapes all the way from the Atlas foothills around Asni to the beautiful panoramas that unfold as you reach the southern face of the range.

Taroudant is an interesting destination and offers a gateway to the magnificent Anti-Atlas Mountains and the beaches of Morocco's deep south. This tour can be completed in a quick two-day escape from Marrakech, but to do the whole region justice, you'll need more time. Bear in mind also that the going can be slower than expected on the mountain roads – the drive from Ouirgane to the top of the Tizi-n-Test, for example, takes at least two hours, while visibility can be hampered (and progress slowed still further) by low cloud. Note that there are no petrol stations between Asni and Olad Berhil.

## LEAVING MARRAKECH

Starting from the roundabout at La Mamounia Hotel, follow the city wall southwards and turn right at the second turning you come to, signposted 'Taroudant'.

*Tin Mal Mosque*

## INTO THE HIGH ATLAS

After about 5km (3 miles), follow the road round to the left (ignoring the right-hand fork to Amizmiz) and continue for a further 29km (18 miles) to **Tahanaoute**, a local administrative town and gateway to the foothills of the High Atlas. Pass through the town, staying on the same road, and follow the winding, mountainous route to the Berber village of **Asni** ❶ (see page 93), some 47km (29 miles) from Marrakech. Asni has a rather intimidating Saturday souk (market), where the locals can get quite pushy, but otherwise it is a reasonable place to stop for a tea break.

Continue through the village, sticking to the main road, where you'll notice a left turn up to the village of Imlil (see page 80). This is a rewarding sidetrip along a scenic 17km (11-mile) road and taking about half an hour in each direction.

### Lunch stop

Back on the Marrakech–Taroudant road, follow the winding section down to the village of **Marigha** (see page 78), continue through the village and look out for a right-hand turn to the French-

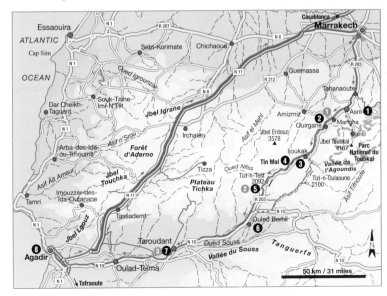

*Stall selling fossils*

owned **La Bergerie** *maison d'hôte*, see ❶, after a further 500m/yds, a good place for lunch.

### Ouirgane

After lunch, continue along the Tizi-n-Test, passing through, after a further 3km (2 miles), the village of **Ouirgane** ❷. Sleepy Ouirgane used to be one of the High Atlas's most appealing villages, although the construction of a dam (of the River N'Fis) has had a major impact on the surrounding physical environment and rather eroded the village's original charm.

### THE N'FIS RIVER VALLEY

Passing through Ouirgane, continue up the Tizi-n-Test. A right-hand bend in the road some 33km (21 miles) from Ouirgane signals your arrival in the village of **Ijoukak** ❸.

#### Off-road options from Ijoukak

To the left, just before the bridge, an unsurfaced track takes you up the beautiful **Agoundis Valley**, where a thin strip of bright cultivation is flanked by towering limestone rock faces, although the track is fairly rough and can occasionally be impassable without a 4x4 vehicle. Those with suitable transport (and some off-road experience) might also consider tackling the superb 72km (45-mile) route down to the Ouarzazate–Taroudant road (N10). To take this route, continue for another 9km (6 miles), cross the river and then climb sharply up to the **Tizi-n-Oulaoune** pass. Stay on the same route south until you eventually arrive at the main road. The scenery is fabulous, but be aware that this route is very remote, and there are no services.

---

## Trips from Taroudant

Taroudant is often used as a springboard for trips further afield. For those with extra time on their hands there are several worthwhile excursions in the region, namely up into the Anti-Atlas Mountains and to the coast.

A strikingly scenic spot with a character all of its own, **Tafraoute** is located some 180km (112 miles) from Taroudant and can be visited as a two-day excursion. Highly recommended is a trip into the mountains, by way of the 'Paradise Valley', to the mountain village of **Imouzzèr-des-Ida-Outanane**, with its waterfall and the Hôtel des Cascades (tel: 0528-82 60 16). To find this road, which winds through picturesque palm oases and mountainside villages, take the coastal road northwards out of Agadir and turn right after 12km (7 miles). From here it is 49km (31 miles) up to the village and hotel. The following day, continue north out of the village until you rejoin the Agadir–Marrakech road (N8). From the junction it takes about two-and-a-half hours back to Marrakech along a fairly major route.

---

Craft shop in an old van

Altitude marker

## Tin Mal

Continuing along the main tarmac route, follow the road through Ijoukak for a further 7km (4.5 miles) before arriving at the Tin Mal mosque, signposted (although not very clearly) to your right. Follow the tarmac road down, over the river and then up to the mosque, where there is an unpaved parking area. You can leave your car with the custodian, who will also let you look around the mosque for around 10–15DH.

**Tin Mal** ❹ was built in 1153 and is one of Morocco's more important historical sites. The 12th-century mosque was the birthplace of the Almohad movement that eventually gave rise to the Berber dynasty of the same name. This mosque, which is roughly contemporary with the Koutoubia (see page 30) in Marrakech, was renovated in the 1990s, having been in an advanced state of decay, and is now one of the few mosques in Morocco that can be visited by non-Muslims. Although the mosque is not currently used by worshippers, there are plans to reopen it in the near future for the collective Friday prayer.

### THE TIZI-N-TEST

After the Tin Mal, the road narrows and eventually winds its way up to the top of the **Tizi-n-Test** ❺ at 2,092m (6,799ft) above sea-level. En route, a few kilometres/miles before the pass, a piste off to the right leads into the heart of the Western High Atlas, a remote and seldom-visited region that is home to the beautiful **Tichka Plateau**.

A four- or five-day trek takes you to the plateau, and down into the villages on the southern side of the watershed, finishing some way north of the town of Ouled Berhil. More isolated, and somewhat less severe in hiking terms, than the Toubkal National Park (see page 80), the Western Atlas offers some interesting possibilities, most of which are best organised in advance from Marrakech.

At the top of the pass, the **Belle Vue Café**, see ❷, offers tea and panoramic views over the Souss plains to the Anti-Atlas Mountains, a more southern parallel range to the High Atlas.

On the south side, improvements to the road (wider bends and crash barriers) have made the Tizi-n-Test much less dangerous than it once was. That said, pay attention to oncoming trucks as you switchback down into the Souss.

### SOUSS VALLEY

From the top of the pass it is 90km (56 miles) to Taroudant. After 37km (23 miles), turn right at the junction with the Ouarzazate–Agadir road and then continue a few kilometres into the rough-and-ready roadside town of **Ouled Berhil** ❻. There's not much of note here apart from the **Riad Hida** (tel: 0528-53 10 44; www.riadhida.

*Agadir beach*

com). Located down a dusty left turn off the main drag, this has 13 comfortable rooms and a pleasant garden plus pool and makes a reasonable overnight stop. Otherwise, continue on through the **Souss Valley** (Vallée du Souss) to Taroudant, which lies a further 44km (27 miles) west on the N10.

### Oranges and lemons

The fertile Souss Valley is one of Morocco's largest citrus fruit-producing areas, with extensive orange and lemon orchards lining the road. The valley is also home to one of the world's rarer tree species – the argan. Only found in southern Morocco and in parts of Mexico, this thorny and rather unsightly species bears a nut that is used in the making of argan oil, used both in Moroccan cuisine and as a massage and treatment oil.

## TAROUDANT

Sitting at the heart of the Souss Valley, in the shadow of some of the finest mountains in Morocco, the walled city of **Taroudant** ❼ is often likened to a miniature Marrakech. Once a temporary seat of government prior to the capture of Marrakech, modern Taoudant is a compact and lively town, which, while rather short on monuments, boasts one of Morocco's most beautifully preserved city walls and some interesting souks. However, the city's medina bears few of the architec-

tural treasures of Marrakech, and many of the buildings in the medina are now modern breeze-block structures.

### The souks

Apart from the rampart, the only historical site of any real interest is the impressive **Bab Kasbah**, a gateway into the city through the eastern wall. The souks themselves have become popular with visitors and now feature on many a coach-tour itinerary from Agadir. This has increased the city's hassle-factor, but there are still some unique crafts on offer as well as a couple of interesting antiques shops.

### Staying overnight

High rollers, royalty, heads of state and celebrities generally choose to stay at the very exclusive hideaway, **La Gazelle d'Or** (tel: 0528-85 20 39; www.gazelle dor.com), tucked away out of time on the south side of the road to Amezgou. A more affordable option is the **Palais Salam Hotel** (tel: 028-85 25 01) on the eastern side of the city wall. This converted 19th-century palace of the then pasha has preserved much of its former splendour: the ground-floor bedrooms even enclose small, luxuriant gardens.

Taroudant is not big on restaurants, bars or nightlife, so you may decide to eat your evening meal in the hotel itself; otherwise, try the **Riad Dar Zitoune**, see ❸, which also offers accommodation (see page 109).

*Taroudant's city walls*                    *Taroudant musicians*

## RETURN TO MARRAKECH

For those heading back to Marrakech from Taroudant on day two, either retrace your journey back over the Tizi-n-Test, or take the geographically longer, but quicker and easier, route via Agadir on the Agadir–Marrakech road, the N8, which also offers the chance of seeing an alternative view of the countryside hereabouts.

### Agadir
Following a catastropic earthquake in 1960, **Agadir ❽** was completely rebuilt and is now Morocco's premier beach resort, with 10km (6 miles) of broad sandy beach and an average of 300 days of sunshine a year. Conceived as a showcase for modern Morocco, it has no ancient medina or tempting souks, but it does have tourist shops, restaurants, hotels and international-style tourist complexes aplenty – and as many tourists as the rest of the country put together. One of the few remaining historic monuments is the **kasbah** – at the northern end of the bay – from which there are superb views down on to the port and the city.

Agadir is an example of full-throttle, commercial Morocco, but the city has a number of good restaurants on the seafront, which make it an ideal stop-off point before embarking on the 238km (149-mile) journey back to Marrakech, which now only takes 2.5 hours, since the highway opened in 2010.

## Food and Drink

### ❶ LA BERGERIE
Marigha, Route du Tizi-n-Test; tel: 0524-48 57 17; €€

Provençal-style guesthouse with Moroccan and French food served on its patio, with views of the surrounding hills.

### ❷ BELLE VUE CAFÉ
Summit of the Tizi-n-Test; no tel.; from 8am; €

This café/budget hotel, which offers some of the best views in Morocco from its terrace, makes an excellent stop for a refreshment break. There isn't a great deal of food on offer (just a handful of snacks), but they can rustle up an omelette, if you arrive in need of a meal. There is another café of the same name on the north side of the pass, but its views are not as good.

### ❸ RIAD DAR ZITOUNE
Boutariat El Berrania, Taroudant; tel: 028-55 11 41; www.darzitoune.com; daily; €€€

Situated on the edge of town (on the road to Agadir), this hotel-restaurant is one of the best eating options in Taroudant. Choose from a selection of international dishes served either in the attractive poolside garden or in the sunny dining room decorated in local style.

# DIRECTORY

Hand-picked hotels and restaurants to suit all budgets and tastes, organised by area, plus select nightlife listings, an alphabetical listing of practical information, a language guide and an overview of the best books and films to give you a flavour of the city.

*La Sultana terrace*

# ACCOMMODATION

If your heart is set on staying in a riad, be aware that they vary tremendously, from a simple guesthouse with two or three rooms to stylish boutique hotels offering every luxury. There are several websites that specialise in booking riad accommodation; you can normally book a room, suite or a whole riad. For a range of riads in the northern part of the medina, try Marrakech Riads (www.marrakech-riads.net).

Quoted prices in all hotels and riads are sometimes subject to a small tourist tax of around 20DH per night. You should also be sure to clarify whether the rate you are quoted includes breakfast or if this will be an extra charge. You may prefer to pay less and have breakfast in a café nearby, especially in the Ville Nouvelle where good cafés are abundant.

In spite of so many new hotels and riads having opened in recent years, it is essential to book accommodation in advance, especially during busy periods such as Easter and Christmas. If you do find yourself in Marrakech without pre-booked accommodation, your best bet is to investigate the many small to medium modern hotels in side streets off Avenue Mohammed V in Guéliz.

## The Medina

### Les Borjs de la Kasbah
Rue du Méchouar; tel: 0524-38 11 01; www.lesborjsdelakasbah.com; €€€
Located in the northern Kasbah, this comfortable spa-hotel was converted from an old riad. The spacious double and superior rooms (plus some singles) are situated around a series of courtyards. Facilities include a good little restaurant, a heated pool concealed behind high red walls, and a spa and hammam in one of the watchtowers.

### Casa Lalla
16 Derb Jemaa, off Rue Riad Zitoun el Kdim; tel: 0524-42 97 57; www.casalalla.com; €€
This stylish riad in the southern part of the medina has eight rooms, each with its own special feature such as a private terrace, fireplace or mezzanine sleeping area. The rooms are comfortably and tastefully furnished, and all have chic and luxurious bathrooms. It is worth coming to Casa Lalla for the food alone – a *menu dégustation* (also open to non-residents) is served at 8pm every evening.

> Price for a double room for one night in high season. Includes breakfast unless otherwise stated:
> €€€€ = Over €200 (2,200DH)
> €€€ = €100–200 (1,100–2,200DH)
> €€ = €50–100 (550–1,100DH)
> € = under €50 (550DH)

*Jnane Tamsna*

## Dar Attajmil

23 Rue Laksour; tel: 0524-42 69 66;
www.darattajmil.com; €€€

A magical riad set around a leafy courtyard, with four individually decorated,
en-suite rooms. It's owned by an Italian
lady who has excellent advice on things to
do in Marrakech and surrounding areas.
Cooking classes are also available.

## Dar Fakir

16 Derb Abou el Fadail, off Riad
Zitoun el Jedid; tel: 0524-441 100;
www.darfakir.co.uk; €€

From the same owner Nourdine Fakir,
who runs some trendy venues in Marrakech, including Villa Rosa and Nikki
Beach (great for hip daytime lounging),
this small riad, with just 8 rooms, caters
for the clubbing generation. The simple
but stylish rooms are set around a great
courtyard strewn with cushions. The
heady incense burns non-stop, and the
Buddha Bar lounging music adds to the
chilled atmosphere.

## Dar el Souk

56 Derb Jdid; tel: 0524-39 15 68;
www.darelsouk.com/riad; €€

Located in a great part of the medina just
steps from Jemaa el Fna, this immensely
popular flower-filled riad has individually
decorated rooms with private outside
seating areas, plus terrific views from
the two cushion-covered roof terraces.

## Dar Soukaina

19 Derb el Farrane; tel: 0524-37 60 54;
www.darsoukaina.com; €

A blissfully peaceful, simply decorated little riad with charming rooms set around
two lovely courtyards shaded by a huge
orange tree. There's also a secluded roof
terrace and a Berber tent. Dinner available on request.

## Dar Tchaikana

25 Derb el Ferrane; tel: 0524-38 51 50;
www.tchaikana.com; €€

It's all about attention to detail at this
super-stylish and consistently recommended riad. The members of staff are
as welcoming and discreet as the décor,
and the food is excellent.

## Dar Warda

266 Derb Sidi Bouamor, Riad Lâarouss;
tel: 0524-37 83 56; www.darwarda.com;
€€€

In the northern half of the medina, this
intimate and tastefully furnished riad
has just five sumptuously decorated
suites set around a central patio and
picture-perfect pool.

## Hotel Essaouira

3 Sidi Bouloukate; tel: 0524-44 38 05;
€

One of the best of the dozens of little
guesthouses dotting the honeycomb
of alleys south of the Jebel el Fna. The
rock-bottom prices (just 100DH a night
for a double), attractive rooms and helpful staff make this a popular choice for
budget travellers. Advance bookings are
strongly recommended. Note that – as in

*Riad el Fenn courtyard*

many of the city's budget hotels – credit cards are not accepted.

## Hotel Gallia

30 Rue de la Recette; tel: 0524-44 59 13; €
Attractive, comfortable and relatively inexpensive rooms arranged around a traditionally tiled courtyard with a palm tree in the middle. Well situated off Rue Bab Agnaou, near the Jemaa el Fna. Book ahead.

## Hotel Sherazade

Derb Riad Zitoun el Kdim; tel: 0524-42 93 05; www.hotelsherazade.com; €
Popular small hotel, based around two riads with plant-filled courtyards and good rooftop terraces. Most of the 22 rooms are en-suite, some also have air conditioning, but there are also a few super-cheap doubles with shared bathrooms.

## Les Jardins de la Medina

Derb Chtouka; tel: 0524-38 18 51; www.lesjardinsdelamedina.com; €€€€
A huge riad converted into a comfortable hotel with lush walled gardens, beautiful pool and hammam, and a top-notch restaurant (plus in-house cooking school). The décor is modern Moorish with clean lines and bold designs. Most rooms have fireplaces, and superior rooms also have terraces.

## La Maison Arabe

1 Derb Assehbe; tel: 0524-38 70 10; www.lamaisonarabe.com; €€€€
Beautiful riad hotel, full of antiques, with elegant rooms and lots of cosy places to sit. There's also a fine-dining Moroccan restaurant and one of the city's best cookery schools, plus spa and pool.

## Riad 72

72 Arset Awsel; tel: 0524-38 76 29; www.riad72.com; €€€
Perfectly designed boutique riad close to Bab Doukkala, with just four grand rooms. The roof terrace is one of the highest in the medina and has wonderful views and complete privacy.

## Riad Akka

65 Derb Lahbib Magni, off Rue Riad Zitoun el Jedid; tel: 0524-37 57 67; www.riad-akka-marrakech.com; €€
Akka is what the last oasis before the caravan reaches the Sahara is called, and this small guesthouse with just five rooms truly is in an oasis in this hectic city. Designed by the owner, a French interior designer, this sleek riad successfully mixes a contemporary style with the rich traditional Moroccan heritage, but the overall effect is always sensuous. Freshly prepared meals can be ordered in advance.

## Riad Dar More

44 Derb Jdid, Rue Riad Zitoun el Kdim; tel: 0524-661 39 86 20; www.riad-dar-more.com; €€
Charming riad offering a calm oasis in the centre of the city just five minutes' walk from the Jemaa el Fna. It's been

*Riad el Fenn*                                    *Skyline view*

furnished with contemporary flair by its French owner, Dominique, and the rooms are all at very competitive rates.

## Riad Farnatchi
2 Derb el Farnatchi; tel: 0524-384910; www.riadfarnatchi.com; €€€€
This riad fit for a movie star is an exercise in discreet luxury. The nine suites are sumptuously huge yet cosy, with sunken baths and terraces where you can eat your breakfast to the sound of birdsong. A place to stay that earns every dirham of its price tag.

## Riad el Fenn
Derb Moullay Abdullah Ben Hezzian, Bab el Ksour; tel: 0524-44 12 10; www.riadelfenn.com; €€€€
Decadent bohemian luxury spread over four riads knocked into one, with 21 uniquely designed suites, three pools, a bar and two restaurants. The spectacular roof terrace with plunge pool lies in the shadow of the Koutoubia Mosque, and there's also a spa, library, movie room and organic garden.

## Riad Magi
79 Derb Moulay Abdel Kader, Dabachi; tel: 0524-42 66 88; www.riad-magi.com; €€
An attractive and intimate riad, situated east of the main souks, offering six en-suite rooms decorated in vibrant North African colours. There is also a pleasant roof terrace. Breakfast is included, and other meals can be ordered by arrangement.

## Riad l'Orangeraie
61 Rue Sidi el-Yamani; tel: 0524-37 87 89; www.riadorangeraie.com; €€€
One of the medina's most alluring riads, with great staff, a tranquil atmosphere, good breakfasts and Moroccan-style rooms in pale colours set around a courtyard with a swimming pool.

## Riad Porte Royale
84 Derb el Maada, Diour Jdad; no. tel – contact by email on riadporteroyale@gmail.com; www.riadporteroyale.com; €€€
Lovingly restored by an English writer, Riad Porte Royale provides a calm oasis in the spiritual heart of the medina. It is filled with antiques and textiles from all over the world and with a pretty tiled plunge pool in the courtyard.

## Riad Safar
29 Derb Ouihah, Quartier Sidi Abdelaziz; tel: 0524-39 10 10; www.riad-safar.com; €€
This four-room riad is decorated in sumptuous traditional style and is a peaceful haven tucked away in the medina, a short walk from the Jemaa el Fna. Staff are helpful and welcoming.

## Riad W
41 Derb Boutouil; tel: 0665-36 79 36; www.riadw.com; €€€
Minutes from Jemaa el Fna is one of the most stylish riads in the medina. Riad W is the height of simplicity with a fashionable and modern feel with stripped-back wooden doors and exposed brickwork, carefully placed antiques

*La Sultana*

and stylish pieces of furniture. The rooms are cosy, there is a little plunge pool in the courtyard and the roof terrace is a lovely place to unwind and have breakfast or lunch.

### Riyad el Cadi

87 Derb Moulay Abdelkader, Dabachi; tel: 0524-37 86 55; www.riyadelcadi.com; €€€

This large riad just east of the main souks comprises 12 rooms and suites leading off five patios. The rooms feature antique textiles, and there is a small pool and a pleasant roof terrace. The self-contained 'Blue House', which is equipped with its own kitchen and patio, is ideal for private hire.

### Royal Mansour

Rue Abou Abbas el Sebti; tel: 0524-80 80 80; www.royalmansour.com; €€€€€

One of the most spectacular – and spectacularly expensive – hotels in the country, built by Mohammed VI to celebrate the very best in Moroccan design and craftsmanship. Accommodation is in one of 53 private riads, each with its own plunge pool and sitting room. There's exceptional dining at one of the three restaurants, with almost 100 chefs in attendance.

### La Sultana

403 Rue de la Kasbah; tel: 0524-38 80 08; www.lasultanahotels.com/marrakech; €€€€

Ornate luxury hotel with a good location near the Saadian Tombs. A complex of four riads offers 28 spacious rooms and suites, an attractive heated pool and a well-equipped spa with an open-air jacuzzi on its roof. The décor may be a little over the top for many people's taste, but it's wonderfully exotic for others.

### Tlaatawa Sitteen

63 Derb el Ferrane; tel: 0524-38 30 26; €

Great budget option run by a charming Moroccan family. The traditional riad houses six simple but stylish rooms with shared tadelakt bathrooms. Dinner is available on request.

### Villa Flore

4 Derb Azzouz; tel: 0524-39 17 00; www.villa-flore.com; €€

Small boutique hotel in the Mouassine quarter. Each of the five rooms is individually furnished in a fresh, modern style, with a well-equipped bathroom. The hotel also has a good restaurant. Half-board rates are available.

### Villa des Orangers

6 Rue Sidi Mimoun; tel: 0524-38 46 38; www.villadesorangers.com; €€€€

Located not far from the Jemaa el Fna, this established hotel successfully incorporates modern comforts (large, sleek beds and luxuriously appointed bathrooms) into a traditional but tasteful setting with antique furniture, open fires in winter, a good-size pool and excellent restaurant. One of the city's top addresses.

*Bedroom in Riad Magi*

*Pool at Les Borjs de la Kasbah*

## Guéliz and the Hivernage

### Diwane Hotel

Rue de Yougoslavie; tel: 0524-43 22 16; www.diwane-hotel.com; €€

A no-frills, reasonably priced four-star hotel just off Place Abdel Moumen Ben Ali in the centre of the Ville Nouvelle, with decent-sized rooms and a good pool. Ideal for families.

### Hotel Toulousain

44 Rue Tarik Ben Ziad; tel: 05 24 43 00 33, www.hoteltoulousain.com; €

A long-running budget hotel in the heart of the Ville Nouvelle. Simple, good-value rooms (some with shared bathrooms) are set around a pair of attractive courtyards. The peaceful atmosphere and friendly staff offer a welcome respite after a day navigating the souks.

### La Mamounia

Avenue Bab Jdid; tel: 0524-38 86 00; www.mamounia.com; €€€€

The Grand Old Lady of Marrakech, between the medina and Guéliz, combining old-world-style with modern five-star luxuries. All rooms have views of the magnificent gardens and Atlas Mountains. Following a three-year, multi-million-pound restoration, the hotel is now in sparkling form. Pure Art Deco lingers on in the leather- and wood-panelled Le Bar Churchill, named after La Mamounia's most famous patron, Britain's wartime prime minister, keen amateur painter and ardent Moroccophile Winston Churchill, who visited on several occasions during his retirement in order to capture the city on canvas. Facilities include four restaurants – Moroccan, Italian, French and seafood – five bars, a spa and a casino (www.grandcasinomamounia.com). The hotel's bars and restaurants (Le Pavillon de la Piscine by the pool and the traditional Le Marocain riad-style restaurant) are open to non-guests, meaning that it's possible to experience something of the hotel's time-warped luxury even if you can't afford to stay here. Smart dress is advised.

## The Palmeraie

### Les Deux Tours

Douar Abiad; tel: 0524-32 95 25; www.lesdeuxtours.com; €€€€

One of the oldest and most beautiful hotels in the Palmeraie. Built by Tunisian architect Charles Boccara as his private home, the jungle-style gardens are beautiful, the pool sublime, and the rooms are all unique (some have their own private pools). Understated luxury in a wonderfully romantic setting.

### Jnane Tamsna

Douar Abiad; tel: 0524-32 93 40; www.jnanetamsna.com; €€€

Set in stunning organic gardens, with 24 secluded and sumptuous suites spread over three houses that feel like your own private homes. Amenities include two pools, an opulent salon, tennis courts and lush gardens, where organic produce for the kitchen is grown.

*Villa des Orangers*

### Ksar Char Bagh

Djnan Abiad; tel: 0524-32 92 44;
www.ksarcharbagh.com; €€€€

This exquisite hotel, set in large, pristine gardens, has some of the best food in Marrakech and one of the most decadent hammams. It also has its very own London black cab, a 34m (112ft) heated pool, and a wonderful library with over a thousand books.

### Palmeraie Golf Palace

Circuit de la Palmeraie; tel: 0524-334 334;
www.pgpmarrakech.com; €€€€

Vast luxury complex, with eight restaurants, five pools, a fitness centre and horse riding, attached to superb 18-hole golf course. Also hosts Nikki Beach, for daytime lounging, and Dar Ennasim restaurant (see page 118), run by chef Fabrice Vulin.

### Outskirts of Marrakech

### Amanjena

Route de Ouarzazate, Km 12; tel: 0524-40 35 53; www.amanjena.com; €€€€€

The first Aman resort in Africa is situated 12km (7 miles) south of Marrakech on the Ouarzazate road. The ultimate in luxury, it comprises palatial pavilions set among palm and olive trees; some have their own pools and butler service. Every amenity you could desire, at similarly exalted prices.

### Beldi Country Club

Route du Barrage, Km 6; tel: 0524-38 39 50; www.beldicountryclub.com; €€€

A wonderful retreat, set in extensive rose gardens 15 minutes' drive from Marrakech. Rooms are decorated in rustic style and there's a fabulous pool and great artisanal workshops in the attached 'souk' where you can buy pottery, linens and carpets.

### La Pause

Douar Lmih Laroussiene, Commune Agafay; tel: 0661-30 64 94; www.lapause-marrakech.com; €€€

Rustic rooms in mudbrick with a simple but warm and comfortable décor. This is the perfect place to come for a respite from Marrakech city life, even for the afternoon or evening, but it is better for a longer stay. The hotel organises dinners by the fire, or sessions of cross golf, mountain biking, walking and horse riding to discover its amazing surroundings with the High Atlas peaks as a backdrop. No electricity, but this makes for some exceptional desert skies at night.

### Villas Fawakay

Off Route de Ouarzazate, Km 8; tel: 0673 18 73 46; www.fawakayvillas.com; €€€

Hidden away down a dusty road, this unusual place, run by an English expat family who live on site, consists of three large, stylish villas in verdant gardens with a pool. It combines privacy with the ease of a hotel, as meals are all catered for – there's a nightly menu of delicious dishes. Minimum two-night stay.

*Dar Qamar*

## Essaouira

### Auberge Tangaro

4km (2 miles) south of Essaouira, on the way to Diabet; tel: 0524-78 47 84; www.aubergetangaro.com; €€

Located a few kilometres outside Essaouira, this renovated hotel offers a marvellously oceanfront retreat a short drive from the city, with 18 bright and attractively decorated rooms set in lovely gardens with Atlantic views.

### Heure Bleu

2 Rue Ibn Batouta; tel: 0524-78 34 34; www.heure-bleu.com; €€€

Essaouira's finest hotel has gracious rooms and suites that are beautifully decorated in styles bearing African, oriental and British colonial influences. There is a stunning rooftop pool with views over the city, a private cinema, a billiard room and a spa that includes a massage room with wraparound views.

### Hôtel Beau Rivage

145 place Moulay Hassan; tel: 0524-47 59 25; www.beaurivage-essaouira. com; €

Refurbished classic Essaouira budget hotel, as central as it gets, overlooking the place Moulay Hassan. Rooms are squeaky clean and comfortable, and breakfast is served on the roof terrace.

### Madada Mogador

5 Rue Youssef el Fassi; tel: 0524-47 55 12; www.madada.com; €€€€

Ultra-chic riad on the edge of the medina. Most of the (large) rooms have private terraces overlooking the port and are decorated in a cool contemporary style.

### Riad Loulema

2 Rue Souss; tel: 0524-47 53 46; www.darloulema.com; €€

All is light and calm in this stunning 18th-century riad, located just off the ramparts. The rooms are named after places in Morocco and decorated accordingly. Fabulous food is available on request.

### Villa Maroc

10 Rue Abdellah Ben Yassine; tel: 0524-47 61 47; www.villa-maroc.com; €€€

One of Morocco's original riad-style guesthouses and still amongst the nicest places to stay in Essaouira. Rooms, all individually designed, are around two courtyards, and there's also a leafy terrace, good food and a hammam. Excellent location not far from the main square, and with views over the seafront.

## The High Atlas

### Au Sanglier Qui Fume

Tel: 0524-48 57 07; www.ausanglier quifume.com; €

Characterful auberge with a hugely popular restaurant serving Franco-Moroccan cuisine (in the summer on a vine-shaded terrace, in winter in a cosy dining room). Lots of activities are on offer – from mountain biking to boules.

*Palmeraie Golf Palace*

## La Bergerie

Ouirgane; tel: 0524-48 57 17;
€€

This stone lodge decorated in traditional Berber style is situated amid some outstanding countryside. It offers simple but comfortable rooms (some with fireplace), a cosy restaurant and bar, and an outdoor pool in summer.

## Chez Juju

Oukaimeden; tel: 0524-31 90 05;
www.hotelchezjuju.com; €€

This wonderful chalet-style lodge is the nicest place to stay in Oukaimeden with charming rooms and a wonderful restaurant serving warming casseroles – always full on snowy weekends.

## Dar Adrar

Imlil (60km/40 miles from Marrakech);
tel: 0668-76 01 65/0670-72 68 09;
www.daradrar.com; €

This is a simple but delightful guesthouse, perched on top of the village, run by one of the most expert mountain guides in the area, Mohammed Aztat. He can also arrange hikes in the Atlas.

## Dar Imlil

Imlil; tel: 0524-48 56 11;
www.kasbahdutoubkal.com; €€€

This small hotel is set in some lovely countryside some 10 minutes from the centre of Imlil. There's a great terrace overlooking the valley, and simple but comfortable rooms with en-suite facilities.

## Domaine de la Roseraie

Ouirgane; tel: 0524-43 91 28;
www.laroseraiehotel.com; €€

Long-established mountain retreat with 40 rooms and four suites (the latter with their own fireplaces), set in the midst of lovely gardens. There is a good restaurant, plus three pools and a hammam, and horse riding and trekking with mules can be arranged.

## Douar Samra

Imlil: tel: 0524-48 40 34; www.douar-samra.com; €€

Tranquil Berber lodge 2km (1.25 miles) up a dirt track from Imlil, with cosy rustic rooms, a tree house, traditional wood-burning hamman and stupendous views over the Atlas Mountains.

## Irocha

Douar Tisselday, Ighrem N'Oudal; tel: 0667-73 70 02; www.irocha.com; €

Delightful guesthouse, with simple but lovingly decorated rooms, using textiles and furnishings collected on trips across Morocco. Geologist Ahmed was born in the village nearby, and Catherine has lived in the country for many years. Together they offer the warmest welcome, interaction with the local culture, interesting walks and delicious French-Moroccan meals supervised by Catherine, who is an excellent cook.

## Kasbah Bab Ourika

Tel: 0668-74 95 47, www.kasbahbabourika.com; €€€

Set in landscaped gardens on its own hilltop, with 360-degree views, this idyllic kasbah hotel has luxurious rooms and a wonderful pool. Lots of activities available, including trekking, skiing, mountain-biking and various day-trips.

### Kasbah Tamadot

Route d'Imlil; tel: 0524-36 82 00; www.kasbahtamadot.virgin.com; €€€€

Richard Branson spotted this hilltop kasbah while hot-air ballooning here. He subsequently bought the property and transformed it into a luxury retreat with gorgeous Arabian Nights-style suites and very upmarket Berber tents, plus spa treatments, guided treks and day trips to Marrakech.

### Kasbah du Toubkal

Imlil; tel: 024-48 56 11; www.kasbahdutoubkal.com; €€€

This stunning kasbah hotel has a variety of accommodation and is the best place to base yourself for treks up Jebel Toubkal. It's also run in partnership with the local Berber community, meaning that a percentage of all revenues goes to the village association.

### Riad Dar Zitoune

Boutarial El Berrania, Taroudant; tel: 028-55 11 41; www.darzitoune.com; €€€

An attractively rustic option, with a mix of Berber and Moorish décor and a pleasant pool set in a verdant garden. Offers a range of rooms and suites.

## Agdz and Ouarzazate

### Dar Daïf

Talmasla, Ouarzazate; tel: 0524-85 49 47; www.dardaif.ma; €€€

Rambling, rustic and eco-friendly kasbah-style hotel on the outskirts of town overlooking the Palmeraie. It's attractively decorated with local crafts, and there's also a private hammam plus a wide range of activities and tours.

### Dar Qamar

Kasbah Agdz, Agdz; tel: 0524-84 37 84; www.locsudmaroc.com; €€

A corner of the Agdz Kasbah now converted into a mid-range hotel with comfortable, if simply furnished, rooms, a restaurant and pool. There's also an attractive tented area for lounging under the stars in the evening.

## Agadir

### Hotel Atlantic

Avenue Hassan II; tel: 0528-84 36 61; http://atlantichotelagadir.com; €€

Appealing three-star resort with attractive rooms and more facilities than you'd expect at the price, including a private section of beach, spa and a pretty little pool.

### Riad Villa Blanche

Baie des Palmiers, Bensergao; tel: 0528-21 13 13; www.riadvillablanche.com; €€€

One of the top hotels in town, this beautiful boutique riad-style hotel is set close to the beach, with 28 rooms, plus a pool, spa and library.

*Aubergines and peppers*

# RESTAURANTS

In Marrakech, as everywhere else, the wise advice if you want to sample simple traditional food is to eat where local people eat. At the higher end of the price spectrum there are several wonderful places that reflect the rich range of Moroccan cooking itself, often producing modern twists on traditional dishes or creating huge feasts fit for a king – starting with a pastilla and ending, several courses later, with honey and nut encrusted halwa or exotically spiced fruit. Several grand riads and palaces in the medina offer such gourmet set menus in magnificently exotic surroundings. The food is good, albeit expensive by Moroccan (and even international) standards and most people can only do it once – the majority find it hard to get beyond the third course.

Be aware that Moroccans tend to eat later than northern Europeans. Restaurant opening times resemble those of southern Europe, with lunch taken between 1pm and 3pm, and dinner served from 8pm until around

11pm. The swisher restaurants in the medina tend to open for dinner only, so for lunch you're advised to head to the Ville Nouvelle, where restaurants cater to a mixed crowd of tourists and local office workers.

The growth of tourism, and general affluence, in Marrakech has made the city an increasingly popular place to eat out, so you are advised to make reservations at most of the restaurants listed. You can usually find a table at lunchtimes, but in the evenings the city's more popular restaurants can be very crowded.

## The Medina

### Café Arabe

184 Rue el Mouassine; tel: 0524-42 97 28, www.cafearabe.com; €€€

Serving both Italian and Moroccan food, this popular restaurant has seating both in a courtyard and on a stunning roof terrace with superb medina views. A great place to stop for lunch or for a romantic dinner.

### Chegrouni

Jemaa el Fna, near Rue des Banques; no tel.; 7am–11pm; €

Simple, long-established restaurant with good views over the eastern periphery of the square. It looks like a tourist trap, but the food isn't too bad, and reasonably priced, with decent bro-

> Price guide for a three-course meal for one, excluding drinks:
> €€€€ = over 500DH
> €€€ = 250–500DH
> €€ = 100–250DH
> € = under 100DH

chettes, harira, lamb chops, kefta, salads and yoghurt. No alcohol.

### Dar Moha

81 Rue Dar el Bacha; tel: 0524-38 64 00; www.darmoha.ma; Tue–Sun dinner only; €€€€

One of the city's most celebrated restaurants, set around a romantic pool in a beautiful villa that once belonged to French fashion designer Pierre Balmain. The menu focuses on modern, inventive Moroccan cuisine – an amazing feast of flavours.

### Dar Yacout

79 Sidi Ahled Soussi; tel: 0524-38 29 29; Mon–Sat dinner only; €€€€

Ranked among Marrakech's finest restaurants, this beautiful medina house, adorned with magnificent stucco and cedar ceilings, serves set menus to satisfy even the most discerning of palates. Delicious salad selections, followed by tajines and couscous, are rounded off with superb Moroccan pastries.

### Dar Zellij

Kaasour Sidi Benslimane; tel: 0524-38 26 27; www.m.darzellij.com; Wed–Mon lunch and dinner; €€€€

If you're staying in the northern medina and you don't fancy the long walk through the souks, then Dar Zellij provides a pleasant option for those in search of Moroccan cuisine in a riad setting. Indoor and outdoor dining options; reservations essential.

### Un Déjeuner à Marrakech

2–4 Place Douar Graoua; tel: 0524-37 83 97; €

This café, tea salon and patisserie in the heart of the medina is a firm favourite with both the locals and with tourists. The food (from spinach and ricotta pies to hamburgers, club sandwiches and salads) is gorgeous, excellent value and great for vegetarians. Sit on the roof terrace if you can.

### Le Foundouk

55 Souk Hal Fassi, Kat Bennahid; tel: 0524-37 81 90; www.foundouk.com; daily lunch and dinner; €€€

Hidden in a maze of alleyways and caravanserais in the northern medina, French-owned Le Foundouk is fashionable and atmospheric, serving excellent French and Moroccan cuisine in a wow-factor setting. Open throughout the day (until late), it is always packed to the rafters.

### Gastro MK

14 Derb Sebaai; tel: 0524-37 61 73; www.maisonmk.com/gastro.htm; dinner only, closed Wed; €€€€

Top-notch Moroccan–French fusion cuisine is showcased here in a fabulous five-course tasting menu featuring fine-dining versions of local classics such as chicken pastilla alongside contemporary European-style dishes. Bookings essential.

*Chicken brochettes*

### Jemaa el Fna foodstalls

Jemaa el Fna; daily dinner only; €

For an authentic experience, pull up a stool with the locals in the Jemaa el Fna square. At these highly animated outdoor eateries expect anything from sheep's heads to snails in a spicy sauce. Less adventurous diners may decide to stick to delicious brochettes (skewers), chips and salad.

### La Maison Arabe

1 Derb Assehbe, Bab Doukkala; tel: 0524-38 70 10; www.lamaisonarabe.com; daily lunch and dinner; €€€€

This hotel has long been renowned for its excellent cooking classes and is also home to 'Le Restaurant', serving perfect Moroccan fare in a gorgeous Moorish setting, and the more colonial-style 'Saveurs d'Ailleurs' restaurant, focusing on world cuisine.

### Mama Ti Lee

13 Derb El Arsa, Riad Zitoun Jdid; tel: 0524-38 17 52; dinner only; €€€

Slightly tricky to find, although you'll be glad you did, and offering the perfect spot for a hideaway-style romantic night out. The cuisine is French, served in a chic contemporary setting with terrace. No alcohol, however. Booking advisable.

### Le Marrakchi

52 Rue des Banques; tel: 0524-44 33 77, www.lemarrakchi.com; noon–midnight; €€€

A more up-market experience than most other cafes hereabouts, but still overlooking the square, with soft furnishings, candlelight, good Moroccan food and alcohol. Wraparound windows offer views of the eastern leg of the square, although equally the glass between you and the action rather neuters the atmosphere.

### Palais Gharnata

5–6 Derb el Arsa, Rue Riad Zitoun el Jdid; tel: 0524-38 96 15; www.gharnata.com; daily lunch and dinner; €€€€

If entertainment in an overblown Moroccan setting with all the orientalist bells and whistles is your thing, then the Palais Gharnata is unlikely to disappoint. In this fiercely traditional palace-style restaurant you can dine on Moroccan cuisine and be entertained by teams of belly dancers and local musicians. Very popular with large tour groups.

### Pepe Nero

17 Derb Cherkaoui; tel: 0524-38 90 67; www.pepenero-marrakech.com; noon to 2.30pm & 7.30–11pm, closed Monday; €€€€

Top-rated restaurant specialising in a mix of classic Moroccan cuisine alongside tempting Italian dishes – mechoui, tagines, and fine home-made pastas – backed up by a quality wine list.

### Le Riad Monceau

7 Derb Chaabane, Riad Zitoun Lakdim;

*Moroccan doughnuts*

tel: 0524-42 96 46; www.riad-monceau.com; €€€

This highly recommended converted riad has a cookery school and particularly fine restaurant, which serves sophisticated and delicate Moroccan dishes in a romantic atmosphere in a courtyard overlooking the riad swimming pool. Bookings usually essential.

## La Sultana

Rue de la Kasbah; tel: 0524-38 80 08; www.lasultanahotels.com; daily dinner only; €€€€

Non-guests are welcomed for dinner at this glorious boutique hotel. There are views over the Saadian Tombs from the roof terrace, and you can dine on specialities such as duck foie gras with apples from Ourika or leg of lamb with honey tajine. Book ahead.

## Tatchibana

38 route de Bab Ksiba, Kasbah; tel: 0524-387 171; www.tatchibana.free.fr; Tue–Sun noon–11pm; €€€

This Japanese restaurant is a testament to how cosmopolitan Marrakech has become. In a peaceful setting, with lots of light, reflected on the white walls and pale wooden furniture, the Tatchibana serves excellent set menus and à la carte Japanese dishes.

## Terrasse des Epices

15 Souq Cherifia; tel: 0524-37 59 04; www.terrassedesepices.com; lunch and dinner; €€

The sister establishment to Café des Epices in the Medina's Spice Market, this fabulous roof-terrace restaurant serves excellent tajines and couscous dishes alongside light European meals, plus a good dessert selection.

## Le Tobsil

22 Derb Moulay Abdellah Ben Hassaien, Bab Ksour R'mila; tel: 0524-44 40 52; Wed–Mon dinner only; closed Aug; €€€€

The well-known Tobsil offers excellent Moroccan food in a beautiful riad that has been lovingly restored by its French owner. The set menu here consists of a number of courses of finely prepared Moroccan staples, all served with grace against a background of traditional *gnaoua* music. The only downside is that it's tricky to find – reserve in advance and staff will come to guide you to the restaurant.

## Toukbal

8 Jemaa el Fna; tel: 024-44 22 62; 7am–midnight; €

This basic café-restaurant on the corner of the square is a great place to sit and watch the world go by amid a mix of locals and foreigners. Try the chicken tagine with preserved lemon, and don't miss the home-made yoghurt.

## Villa Flore

4 Derb Azzouz; tel: 0524-39 17 00; www.villa-flore.com; lunch and dinner; €€€

*Choosing wine at Le Comptoir*

In an elegant converted riad, delicate cuisine is served at sun-shaded tables in a graceful, hidden-away courtyard home. This is just the place to disappear to savour a long lunch and a glass of wine after spending a busy morning in the souks.

## Guéliz and the Hivernage

### Le 6

Avenue Mohammed VI, Hivernage; tel: 0524-44 91 59; daily lunch and dinner; €€

If you are staying in the Hivernage district, Le 6, a bar/bistro, is a reliable local option and popular with expats. It serves well-prepared international staples (pizza, pasta, steak and fish), with both outdoor and indoor dining.

### Le 16

Guéliz Plaza, Guéliz; daily lunch only; €

If you're looking for a light lunch in the heart of the Guéliz shopping district, this popular spot serves good sandwiches and tasty salads and is one of the city's only cafés with a truly modern European feel.

### Al-Fassia

55 Boulevard Zerktouni, Guéliz; tel: 0524-43 40 60; www.alfassia.com; daily dinner only, closed Tue; €€€

One of Marrakech's most popular mid-range Moroccan restaurants, Al-Fassia (run by an all-female team of chefs and waiting staff) serves perhaps the best Moroccan home-cooking in town.

All the favourites take their place on an extensive menu, which includes such delights as chicken with caramelised pumpkin and sweet pigeon pie.

### L'Avenue

Corner of Route de Targa and Rue du Capitaine Arigui; tel: 0524-45 89 01; www.lavenuemarrakech.com; €€€€

High-quality French and Italian cuisine at this swanky bar-restaurant with big chandeliers, leather armchairs and plenty of sparkling wine glasses everywhere.

### Azar

Corner of Rue de Yougoslavie and Boulevard Hassan II; tel: 0524-43 09 20; daily dinner; €€€

This glamorous and romantic restaurant mixes Moroccan, Lebanese and Mediterranean food in a fun and modern way and is usually always full of the city's bright young things. Live shows with belly dancers and orchestra Thur–Sat.

### Bab Hotel

Corner of Boulevard Mansour Eddahbi and Rue Mohamed El Beqal, tel: 0524-43 52 50; daily for breakfast, lunch and dinner; €€€€

The restaurant of the impossibly hip Bab Hotel serves up fantastic Mediterranean-western food. The super-cool, minimalist restaurant gets lively in the evenings, and there is a great Ibiza-style terrace for both lunch and music in the evenings.

*Appetiser, Terrasse des Epices*

*Moroccan pancakes*

### Bagatelle

103 Rue Yougoslavie; tel: 0524-43 02 74;
€€

One of Marrakech's oldest restaurants, this attractively old-fashioned Parisian-style establishment was founded in 1949 and remains popular with locals and expats for its good, solid French food in convivial surroundings.

### Brasserie de Flore

Marrakech Plaza, Place du 16 Novembre; tel: 0524-45 80 00; daily for breakfast, lunch and dinner, until midnight; €€

On the swanky Marrakech Plaza, this bistro serves up fabulously good, classic French food and, unlike many places in town, is very good value for money. Seating in the atmospheric interior (you could be in Paris) or outside with views of the square.

### Brochette Grills Stalls

Rue ibn Aicha, Guéliz; daily lunch and dinner; €

In the street between the Montecristo Café and Rue Casablanca (heralded by the smoke and smell of barbecued meat), a row of simple restaurants with pavement seating serve cuts of meat barbecued in open kitchens. Just select the meat you want at the counter and take a seat. Cheap, fresh and very tasty. Chez Bejgueni is a good option.

### Casanova

221 Avenue Yacoub el Mansour, Guéliz; tel: 0524-42 37 35; daily lunch and dinner; €€

One of the best Italian restaurants in Marrakech, serving high-quality Italian food with its roots in Venetian cuisine. Owned, run and patronised by Italians (a good sign), with indoor and outdoor dining facilities, this simply furnished restaurant offers good value for money and food made with excellent imported ingredients and wines.

### Le Catanzaro

42 Rue Tarik ibn Ziad, Guéliz; tel: 0524-43 37 31; Mon–Sat lunch and dinner, closed Sun; €€

Catanzaro, along with Bagatelle, is arguably the best-known restaurant in the New Town and a popular expat hangout. There's a wide range of moderately priced pizzas and pasta dishes, and the food is unremarkable, but the atmosphere makes the place a one-off. Book ahead.

### Le Chat qui Rit

92 Rue de Yougoslavie, Guéliz; tel: 0524-43 43 11; Tue–Sun dinner; €€

A popular and reasonably priced Franco-Italian backstreet restaurant, with a menu that has enough variety to satisfy most tastes. Recommended for a cheap and unpretentious night out.

### Comptoir Darna

Avenue Echaouada, Hivernage; tel: 0524-43 77 02; www.comptoirmarrakech.com; daily dinner only; €€€€

Probably Marrakech's most famous nightspot, Le Comptoir is as exotic a

*A baker at work*

venue as the city has to offer. It is not noted particularly for its cuisine, but this bar/restaurant serves Moroccan meals to a backbeat of ambient Arabic music, all accompanied by the obligatory belly-dancing floorshow amid beautiful décor. For a group night out Le Comptoir is hard to beat. It's always busy, so it's best to book ahead.

### Le Crystal

Pacha Marrakech, Boulevard Mohammed VI; tel: 0524-38 84 00; www.pachamarrakech.com; daily dinner only; €€€€

The posey Crystal is one of the two places to eat at the mind-boggling Pacha club. It serves its own version of a refined Mediterranean cuisine. Among the delicious options on the menu, tuna carpaccio and *moelleux au chocolat* are some of the chef's specialities.

### La Cuisine de Mona

Résidence Isis, 6 Rue du Capitaine Arrighi; tel: 0618-13 79 59; Mon–Sat lunch and dinner; €€

This friendly, rose-pink restaurant offers tasty Lebanese cooking and mezze that are ideal for snacking on and sharing – the *babaganoush* is highly recommended. There's an attractive small garden, too.

### Le Grand Café de la Poste

Corner of Boulevard Mansour Eddahbi and Avenue l'Imam Malik, Guéliz; tel: 0524-43 30 38; daily from 8am; €€€

The heart of the city's social scene for decades, this brasserie-cum-café occupies the stunning old Art Deco colonial-era post office. Breakfast is served from 8am, followed by light lunches, ice cream, cakes and pastries in the afternoon, and modern French brasserie-style food, with some Moroccan choices, for dinner. Live music most evenings in the lively upstairs bar.

### Le Jacaranda

32 Boulevard Zerktouni, Guéliz; tel: 0524-24 72 15; www.lejacaranda.com; daily lunch and dinner; €€€

Classic French cuisine in the heart of Guéliz. This popular, simple restaurant, which dates back to the 1950s and the era of the Protectorate, is a good bet for well-prepared and tasty food.

### Le Jardin des Arts

6 Rue Sakia El Hamra, Semlalia; tel: 0524-44 66 34; Mon dinner only, Tue–Sat lunch and dinner; €€€

Le Jardin des Arts, situated just off the Casablanca road in Semlalia (north of Guéliz), offers innovative, sophisticated French cuisine served in a modernist Moroccan setting, in an attractive garden. There are good-value menus and à la carte dining.

### Katsura

Rue Oum Errabia; tel: 0524-43 43 58; €€

One of the best Asian restaurants in town, and good value too, serving deli-

*Fresh bread*

cious sushi, maki and other Japanese specialities along with Thai curries, soups and stir-fries.

### Libzar

28 Rue Moulay Ali, tel: 0524-42 04 02; www.libzar.com; Tue–Sun for lunch, daily for dinner; €€€€

This isn't one of the best-known places but scores highly for its inventive, beautifully presented Moroccan food and for its seductively romantic interior.

### Maï Thaï

Villa la Saumuroise, corner of Rue de Paris and Avenue Echouhada, tel: 0524-45 73 01; Tue–Sun, lunch and dinner; €€€€

Considered the best Thai restaurant in town, Maï Thaï is situated in a beautiful Asian-style garden. Its talented chefs produce a delicious blend of Asian and Thai cuisine using only the freshest ingredients. Takeaway and delivery also available.

### Ocha Sushi

43 Rue Yougoslavie, tel: 0524-42 00 88; daily for lunch and dinner; €€

Urban Osha Sushi is a proper sushi bar, with its minimalist green-and-white interest, fresh sushi prepared quickly by the Japanese chef and a refined selection of Japanese teas.

### Palais Jad Mahal

Fontaine de la Mamounia, Hivernage; tel: 0524-43 69 84; www.jad-mahal.com; daily dinner only; €€€

Lavish oriental palace restaurant in the Hivernage offering excellent international/Moroccan fusion cuisine and a floorshow featuring belly dancers and live music. Tasteful and very chic (belly-dancers notwithstanding). Although the food is not especially expensive, a few drinks at the bar can inflate the bill significantly.

### Le Studio

85 Avenue Moulay Rachid; tel: 0524-43 37 00; www.restaurant-lestudiomarrakech. com; dinner Mon–Sat, closed Sun; €€€

One of the best French restaurants in town, this wonderfully low-key but stylish place serves up excellent food including mouth-watering steaks and fresh fish dishes, plus classics including snails, fois gras and parmentier de canard.

### La Table du Marché

Hotel Hivernage, Avenue Haroun Errachid, tel: 0524-42 41 09; www.christophe-leroy.com; daily for lunch and dinner, until midnight; €€

Excellent brasserie, patisserie and tearoom that serves fine French tarts and croissants as well as delicious sandwiches. There is a pretty outside terrace as well.

### La Trattoria de Giancarlo

179 Rue Mohamed Beqal, Gueliz; tel: 0524-43 26 41; www.latrattoriamarrakech.com; dinner daily; €€€€

*Elegant table setting*

In a charming villa that mixes 1920s and Moroccan style, this lovely oasis, with its opulent garden, serves scrumptious Italian cuisine from a menu that travels from Bologna to Tuscany and beyond. Lots of pasta, meat and fish dishes.

## The Palmeraie

### Dar Ennasim

Le Pavillon du Golf, Palmeraie Golf Palace, Circuit de la Palmeraie; tel: 0524-33 43 08; www.fabricevulin.com; daily for lunch and dinner; €€€€

Run by Fabrice Vulin, the proud possessor of two Michelin stars, this is a restaurant for foodies and those celebrating a really special occasion. The restaurant is situated beside a pool on the Palmeraie golf course and has a lovely verandah for dining alfresco. The interior is sleek and modern, with statement furniture and contemporary art on the walls. The delicious modern European food is inventive, often with a Moroccan twist. Fish features prominently on the menu.

## Out of town

### Amanjena

Amanjena Hotel, Route d'Ouarzazate; tel: 0524-40 33 53; daily for lunch and dinner; €€€€

For Thai cuisine and a good look at the interior of one of the most extravagant hotels in Marrakech, head for the restaurant at this hotel in the Amelkis golf complex. The restaurant is situated alongside the swimming pool. Booking essential.

### Bo-Zin

Route de l'Ourika, Km 3.5; tel: 0524-38 80 12; www.bo-zin.com; daily dinner only; €€€

Despite its situation in a nondescript village on the Ourika road (on the edge of town), the dimly lit Bo-Zin is the height of Marrakech chic. It's *the* restaurant for local movers and shakers and a haven of cool that serves a range of specialities from Moroccan to Thai cuisine.

### La Ferme Berbère

Douar Touggana, Route de l'Ourika, Km 9; tel: 0524-38 56 85; www.lafermeberbere.com; daily lunch and dinner; €€

Although it is not especially noted for its fine cuisine, this agreeable spot serves basic Moroccan fare in a grassy garden with a pool and views out to the High Atlas Mountains – a good bet for a long, lazy lunch and a post-lunch lounge. They also do a good Sunday brunch, including use of the pool. Reserve in advance.

### Le Flouka

Barrage Lalla Takerkoust; tel: 0664-49 26 60; www.leflouka.com; €€

A 40-minute drive from Marrakech at the edge of Lake Takerkoust in the shadow of the Atlas. Serves good hearty French food, much of it grilled, at tables set under shady trees and umbrellas next to the water.

*Moroccan snacks*

*Refreshing oranges with cinnamon*

## Le Touggana

Route de l'Ourika, Km 9; tel: 0524-37 62 78; Mon and Wed–Fri dinner only, Sat–Sun lunch and dinner; €€€

Formerly the restaurant 'KM9', Touggana makes for an excellent evening out if you fancy escaping Marrakech for a while. The French-based cuisine is served in an attractive dining room with patio doors that give out on to a bougainvillea-filled terrace. There's also a well-stocked bar for an *apéritif* or *digestif*. Only *grands taxis* will take you this far out of town.

## Essaouira

### After 5

7 Rue Youssef El Fassi; tel: 0524-47 33 49; daily lunch and dinner; €€€

This beautiful restaurant, built into the walls of the medina with tables under traditional stone archways and ambient lighting, serves up the freshest and most delicious fish and seafood in Essaouira as well as excellent French bistro food.

### Elizir

1 Rue d'Agadir; tel: 0524-47 21 03; open evenings only; €€€

Wonderfully quirky Moroccan/Italian restaurant in the heart of the medina decorated with Art Deco flea-market finds and adorned with an eclectic mix of artwork. The short but satisfying menu features a range of fish, pasta and authentic tagines. Extremely popular, so reservations advised.

## Ristorante Silvestro

70 Rue Laalouj; tel: 0524-47 35 55; daily, lunch and dinner; €€€

This well-kept secret is arguably the best Italian restaurant in Morocco and excellent value. Using imported ingredients from Italy and seasonal food and fish from Essaouira's markets, Giuseppe Silvestro and Rhounai Nezha produce mouthwatering, wood-fired pizzas and exquisite pastas and meat dishes. Cash only.

## Taros

Place Moulay Hassan, above Café-Restaurant Marrakech (entrance around the side of the building); tel: 0524-47 64 07; www.taroscafe.com; €€€

This popular bar-restaurant serves excellent Moroccan–French food with a twist. Seating is on a fabulous roof terrace-cum-bar with a relaxed, sunset-in-Ibiza atmosphere, a very mellow soundtrack and sweeping views over the sea and the square.

## Triskala

Rue Touahen; tel: 0655-58 51 31; open evenings only; closed Sun; €€

Bustling Spanish-run café-restaurant in the shadow of the ramparts, occupying an atmospheric little vaulted dining room and serving up a short but excellent selection of daily-changing specials, all beautifully presented and at giveaway prices. There's not much space, however, so arrive early or reserve your table in advance.

# NIGHTLIFE

Traditional Marrakech bars are still male preserves, but there is a growing choice of other places: often bars double up as restaurants, and some cafés serve alcoholic drinks. For live music, any night on the Jemaa el Fna there is *gnaoua* music and dance, and many restaurants have live music with dinner. Check out www.madein-marrakech.com for details of forthcoming events. Admission to clubs ranges from 150–400DH, and includes a drink.

## Music venues

### Dar Cherifa

8 Derb Chorfa el-Kebir; tel: 0524-42 64 63; www.dar-cherifa.com
This fine, restored riad-café (see page 41) hosts occasional concerts and cultural evenings.

### Institut Français

Route de la Targa, outskirts of Guéliz; tel: 0524-44 69 30; www.ifm.ma
Occasional Moroccan or French music concerts, plus exhibitions and film screenings.

### Kechmara

1bis–3 Rue de la Liberté, Guéliz; tel: 0524-42 25 32; Mon–Sat noon–midnight; www.kechmara.com
Popular restaurant and bar, with a live DJ on the upstairs terrace most evenings, when it's usually packed.

### Kosybar

47 Place des Ferblantiers, Southern Medina; tel: 0524-38 03 24; daily 11am–1am; www.kosybar.com
Trendy piano bar with live jazz on weekend evenings and other live bands.

### Taros

Place Moulay Hassan, Essaouira; tel: 0524-47 64 07; Mon–Sat 11am–4pm, 6pm–midnight; www.taroscafe.com
Live music every night on the rooftop terrace at this funky yet chilled place.

### Théâtre Royal

40 Boulevard Mohammed VI, Guéliz; tel: 0524-43 15 16
Splendid outdoor amphitheatre hosting regular theatre and dance productions.

## Bars

### Bo&Zin

Douar Lahna, Route de l'Ourika, 3.5km (2 miles); tel: 0524-38 80 12; daily 8pm–1am or later; http://bo-zin.com
Stylish DJ bar that really gets going after midnight, especially at weekends. Popular outdoor bar in summer.

### Café Arabe

184 Rue Mouassine, Mouassine Quarter; tel: 0524-42 97 28;; daily 10am–midnight; www.cafearabe.com
Atmospheric rooftop and courtyard, where you can relax with a drink.

*Pacha Marrakech*

## Comptoir Darna

Rue Echouhada, Hivernage; tel: 0524-43 77 02; daily 8pm–1am; www.comptoirmarrakech.com
The hippest bar in town. Good for drinks and tapas, as well as a wide choice of cocktails.

## Grand Café de la Poste

Corner of Boulevard Mansour Eddahbi and Avenue Imam Malik, Guéliz; tel: 0524-43 30 38; daily 8am–11pm
The social hub of the Ville Nouvelle. Good for a relaxed drink at any time of day and with an upstairs bar lounge with DJ every evening.

## Terrasse des Epices

15 Souk Cherifia, Dar el Bacha; tel: 0524-37 59 04; daily 10am–midnight; www.terrasse desepices.com
The coolest rooftop bar in the medina, with great music and food.

<h2>Casinos</h2>

## Casino de Marrakesh

Es Saadi Gardens and Resort, Avenue el Kadissia, Hivernage; tel: 0524-44 88 11; daily 8pm–5am; www.essaadi.com
Grand casino located within a swish five-star hotel.

## Grand Casino de la Mamounia

Avenue Bab Jedid, Hivernage; tel: 0524-44 45 70; daily 9pm–6am; www.grandcasino mamounia.com
Splendid Art Deco casino next door to the famous La Mamounia hotel.

<h2>Nightclubs</h2>

## Cantobar

38 Boulevard Moulay Hassan, Guéliz; tel: 0524-43 33 50; daily 7.30pm–4am; www.cantobar-marrakech.com
Bar-restaurant-nightclub with popular karaoke nights. Free if you have dinner and drinks.

## Diamant Noir

Hotel Marrakech, corner Avenue Mohammed V and Rue Oum Errabia, Guéliz; tel: 0524-43 43 51; daily 10pm–4am
Old-fashioned, kitsch nightclub with hip-hop and *Marrakechi* tunes. Gay-friendly on weekday nights. Admission charge.

## Jad Mahal/Le Silver

Rue Haroun Errachid, Hiverage; tel: 0524-43 69 84; www.jad-mahal.com
Choose between the moody lounge bar with live DJ and regular live music acts, or the attached Le Silver nightclub.

## Pacha Marrakech

Boulevard Mohammed VI, Hivernage; tel: 0524-38 84 05; daily 8pm–5am; www.pachamarrakech.com
Enormous complex with several restaurants and lounges. Best at weekends.

## Theatro

Hotel Es Saadi, Avenue el Kadissia, Hivernage; tel: 0524-44 88 11; www.theatromarrakech.com
Long-running club with kitsch theatrical décor, themed nights and special events plus top DJs and regular live music.

*Rooftop view of the city*

# A–Z

## A

### Admission charges

These are very low, usually 10DH for an adult and often free for children. The Majorelle Garden, Ben Youssef Madrassa and Marrakech Museum have higher charges, but these are still relatively inexpensive by European standards.

### Age restrictions

You must be over 21 to hire a car in Morocco, and over 16 to buy alcohol.

## B

### Budgeting

**Accommodation:** An average price for a double room in a reasonable-quality hotel/riad will cost around 1,000–1,500DH, perhaps a little less in low season (mid-summer), but you can stay in a clean but basic hotel for 300DH or less.

**Eating out:** A three-course meal for two with Moroccan wine in a mid-range restaurant will cost about 600DH; a coffee about 15–25DH; and a beer 30–60DH depending on the venue. You can eat in a good but basic grill restaurant for 150DH or less for two.

**Transport:** Hiring a small car for a week costs from around DH3000–3500. Hiring a *grand taxi* and driver for the day costs around 800DH, depending on dis-

tance, often more if organised through your hotel.

## C

### Childcare

Moroccans are very welcoming of children, including in restaurants; however, that may not be the case in some of the foreign-owned riads, so be sure to check this when you book.

Nappies and formula milk are widely available, usually in grocery shops rather than pharmacies, although, if you want a particular brand, it's best to bring it with you, as chances are it won't be available in Marrakech. Some of the larger hotels offer babysitting services.

Most children will find plenty of amusement on the Jemaa el Fna, or taking camel rides in the Palmeraie. Ballooning on a clear day would be an exhilarating treat, too, although there may be a minimum age specified for this, so check with the tour provider in advance. Trips into the desert should also delight children, although be sure to take adequate suncream and water with you, as they may feel the heat even more than adults.

### Climate

The best times to be in Marrakech are late autumn and early spring. Winter

*Riad courtyard*

is usually bright and sunny, and sometimes warm enough to swim, but it can also be cold, especially at night when temperatures can drop to below freezing. Midsummer is usually too hot for doing much apart from lounging by a pool, with temperatures averaging 33°C (91°F) and often rising above 40°C (104°F). If you visit during this period you'll need a hotel with air-conditioning and preferably a pool.

## Clothing

In summer pack light cottons; in winter be sure to take both light clothes for daytime and warm clothing (including a jacket/coat) for the evening.

Remember that Morocco is an Islamic country, so don't wear revealing clothes on the streets. In the evenings, smart-casual is acceptable for most venues, although you won't get into some of the more exclusive hotels, including La Mamounia, wearing jeans.

## Crime

Crime is not especially common, but you should take the usual precautions to try to avoid it: use a safe in your hotel; don't carry too much cash on you; keep an eye on bags and valuables; and don't leave belongings visible in a parked car. At night be sure to park your car in a guarded car park.

If you are the victim of crime, you will need to report it to the police (there is a Tourist Police station on the north side of the Jemaa el Fna) and obtain an offi-cial report to present to your insurer upon your return.

It is inadvisable to buy or use hash-ish. There are many Westerners languishing in Moroccan prisons for drugs offences.

## Customs

The airport Duty Free shop is open to incoming as well as departing passengers. You can take any amount of foreign currency into or out of the country, but must declare on entry amounts over the value of 15,000DH. It is illegal to import or export more than 1,000DH. Duty-free allowances permit the import of 250g tobacco or 200 cigarettes or 25 cigars; one litre of wine plus one litre of spirits; 150ml of perfume and 250ml of eau de cologne.

## Disabled travellers

Facilities for disabled travellers in Morocco are minimal. Only a few top-end hotels have specially adapted rooms, and many cheaper hotels do not have lifts, and so may have limited accessibility. Public transport is also difficult to use for those with impaired mobility – hiring a car is far preferable – while the narrow, crowded and irregular roads of the Marrakech medina also provide significant challenges, and visitors in wheelchairs are likely to be the object of many curious stares. The easiest plan of action is to arrange your journey in advance

*Grands taxis*

with a reputable tour agent – try www.moroccoaccessibletravel.com, who run dedicated accessible tours across the country.

## Driving

It is not worth hiring a car for getting around Marrakech, as taxis are so cheap, and many places are inaccessible by car; it is worth it, however, if you want to get out and see the surrounding region, which is spectacular (especially in the cases of routes 11–14). However, if you only want to go to Essaouira, you are probably better off getting the Supratours or CTM bus, both of which are cheap and efficient (see page 66).

To bring your own car into Morocco you will need Green Card insurance (this can be purchased on arrival at the port in Tangier, if your own insurance company doesn't provide it for Morocco), your vehicle registration document and a European-style photocard licence or international licence.

Petrol stations are plentiful except on routes through the Atlas, where you should be sure to fill up in advance. Forecourt attendants normally fill the tank for you, and may also clean your windscreen and headlamps (small tip welcome but not essential). Most hire cars take lead-free (sans plomb), which is widely available, but be sure to check when you take charge of the car. Petrol costs slightly less than in the UK; more than in the US.

### Car hire

You can book car hire in advance from home using one of the international companies. However, it is often cheaper to arrange something in situ; most companies have offices around Place Abdel Moumen Ben Ali on Avenue Mohammed V. Do try haggling, especially for longer periods. Aside from the usual international companies, such as Avis, Hertz and Europcar, which all have local offices, try these local operators:

**Florida:** tel: 0524-44 42 18; 28 Rue Koutoubia, Marrakech.

**Sweet Tour:** tel: 0524-43 88 34; www.sweet-tour.com.

### Rules of the road

Speed limits are: 40kph (25mph) in urban areas, 100kph (60mph) on the open road, and 120kph (74mph) on motorways (but look out for signs specifying other limits). Be careful to observe these limits: speed-traps are common, especially on approaches to towns. You will receive a small on-the-spot fine for breaking the speed limit. You may also be stopped if front-seat passengers are not wearing a seatbelt.

The old French system of *priorité à droite* (right of way to traffic coming from the right, ie vehicles on a roundabout give way to vehicles coming on to it) is being phased out. However, it is still the case on some roundabouts, so be sure to approach them with care.

As a rule, Moroccans drive quite chaotically but slowly. Dangerous overtak-

*On a motorbike in Guéliz*  *The Tichka Pass*

ing on main roads is common, so again be cautious.

### Breakdown
Your car-hire company should provide you with the number of their breakdown company. Otherwise, flag down a fellow driver and ask for a lift to a repair garage in the nearest town to get assistance.

### Parking
Your riad or hotel will be able to advise on parking. If they don't have their own car park, you will need to park in a public car park or on the street. Either way, a *gardien*, who wears an official badge, will keep an eye on your car for a small charge (5–10DH is sufficient for an hour or two; overnight parking usually costs 15–20DH).

# E

## Electricity
The electricity supply is rated 220 volts in all but the very oldest hotels. Plugs are the round two-pin Continental type, so bring an adaptor if you want to use UK or US appliances.

## Embassies/consulates
### Moroccan embassies
**UK**
49 Queen's Gate Gardens, London SW7 5NE; tel: 020-7581 5001; www.moroccanembassylondon.org.uk.
**US**
1601 21st Street NW, Washington, DC 20009; tel: 202-462 7979; www.embassyofmorocco.us.

### Moroccan consulate
**US**
10 East 40th Street, Floor 23, New York, NY 10016; tel: 212-758 2625; www.moroccanconsulate.com.

### Embassies in Morocco
**British Embassy**
28 Avenue SAR Sidi Mohammed Souissi, Rabat; tel: 0537-63 33 33; www.ukinmorocco.fco.gov.uk.
**US Embassy**
2 Avenue el Fassi, Rabat; tel: 0537-76 22 65; http://morocco.usembassy.gov.

## Emergencies
Emergency telephone numbers are:
Police: **19**
Fire service/ambulance: **15**
There is an office of the Tourist Police on the north side of the Jemaa el Fna.

## Etiquette
In the interests of tourism, *Marrakshis* are fairly tolerant of the behaviour of foreigners, but it is polite to be respectful of Morocco's Muslim culture and avoid wearing revealing clothes in the medina or indulging in overt displays of physical affection (although holding hands is fine). During Ramadan do not eat, drink or smoke on the streets in daylight hours.

Non-Muslims cannot enter working mosques in Morocco.

*Théâtre Royal*

## F

### Festivals

The festival calendar is getting busier year on year, as new festivals are added to boost interest in the city. Some of the main ones are:

**January:** The Marrakech Marathon; www.marathon-marrakech.com.

**March:** Riad Art Expo – art festival staged in the city's many riads.

**April:** International Magic Festival – Marrakech hosts the largest magic festival in the world, with artists from all corners performing for four days.

**June:** Essaouira's Gnaoua Music Festival takes over the town; www.festival-gnaoua.net.

**July:** The Festival National des Arts Populaires de Marrakech takes place at El Badi Palace, celebrating local folklore; www.marrakechfestival.com.

**December:** International Film Festival – held in early December in the Palais des Congrès, the Théâtre Royal and various smaller venues. A giant screen is erected on the Jemaa el Fna's western side; www.festivalmarrakech.info.

## G

### Gay travellers

Morocco no longer offers visitors the free and easy attitude it once did towards homosexuality. What Moroccan law describes as an 'unnatural act' between two persons of the same sex is punishable by imprisonment (from six months to three years) and by fines, although the law is only loosely enforced, and you're unlikely to run into trouble assuming you're discreet. It's also not generally a problem for same-sex couples to share a hotel room, although again discretion is the order of the day. It is also important to approach gay encounters with Moroccans with caution; it could be a set-up or there may be an economic motive. That said, Marrakech has long been a centre for expatriate male homosexuality, and many foreign-owned riads offer discreet places to stay.

## H

### Health

No vaccinations are required for entry into Morocco unless you have come from a yellow fever, cholera or smallpox zone. If you need to see a doctor or dentist during your stay in Morocco, staff in your hotel/riad will be able to assist in finding one.

### Insurance

All medical care must be paid for so be sure to take out adequate health insurance before you travel.

### Stomach upsets

These are easily avoided, if a few simple precautions are taken: don't eat food that has been left standing or reheated, peel fruit, treat salads with circumspection and only drink bottled

*Dentist's sign in the souk*                              *Cyber Parc*

water. If you are struck down, drink plenty of water, preferably with rehydration salts, and take a diarrhoea remedy (available at pharmacies). An interesting local remedy for upset stomachs is cactus fruit, also known as Barbary fig. You will see it being sold from stands on street corners. For a few dirhams the vendor will peel one or two for you while you wait.

## Hours and holidays

### Business hours
**Shops in the medina:** Sat–Thur 10am–8pm, some also open Fri.
**Shops in Guéliz:** Mon–Sat 10am–7.30pm (sometimes closing for an hour or two at lunch), closed Sun.
**Banks:** Winter: Mon–Fri 8am–noon and 2–4pm; Ramadan: Mon–Fri 9.30am–3pm.

### State holidays
**New Year's Day:** 1 Jan
**Independence Manifesto Day:** 11 Jan
**Labour Day**: 1 May
**Feast of the Throne:** 30 July
**Oued Ed Dahab (Reunification Day):** 14 Aug
**Revolution Day:** 20 Aug
**Anniversary of the Green March:** 6 Nov
**Independence Day:** 18 Nov

### Muslim holidays
These are governed by the Hegira lunar calendar and are therefore movable. The holidays get earlier by about 11 days each year (12 in a leap year). Exact dates depend on the sighting of the new moon.
**Mouloud:** The Prophet's birthday. In 2015 this falls on 2 January.
**Aid es Seghir:** (marking the end of Ramadan). 18 June in 2015.
**Aid el Kebir:** (feast of Abraham's sacrifice of a lamb instead of his son). 5 October in 2014; 24 September in 2015.
**Muslim New Year:** 25 October 2014, 15 October 2015.

# I

## Internet

There are numerous internet cafés, and some *téléboutiques* also offer internet access. Internet access costs around 10DH an hour. WiFi is now increasingly widespread, with almost all hotels (and many cafés) offering it free to guests.

# M

## Maps

A free map is available from the tourist office (see page 130), but its coverage of the complex souk area is sketchy.

In addition to the map found in the back of this book, the best available maps are *Insight FlexiMap Marrakech*, published by Apa Publications (www.insightguides.com); the *Marrakech: Medina Street Plan* by Medinacarte.com, showing the old city in exceptional detail; and *Marrakech & Essaouira* pub-

*Magazine stand*

lished by Editions Laure Kane. Michelin map no. 742 covers the whole of Morocco and features an enlargement of Marrakech.

In the UK, these are most easily available from the travel book and map specialist Stanfords (12–14 Long Acre, London WC2, and 29 Corn Street, Bristol BS2; www.stanfords.co.uk; orders can be placed online), as well as other good bookshops.

## Media

### Publications

There is a range of daily and weekly publications in French and Arabic. The two main publications in French are the pro-Royal *Le Matin* and the more liberal *L'Opinion*. Weeklies include *Le Journal* and the outspoken *TelQuel*. *Le Monde* is also widely available, as are some English newspapers, but the latter will be at least a day old by the time you buy them – better to read them online.

For listings of forthcoming events visit www.madein-marrakech.com and click on the 'Events' button.

### Television

Most hotels provide CNN and BBC World satellite channels. Morocco has two state-run TV channels, 2M and TVM, which are more interesting than they used to be, providing that you can understand French or Arabic, but far from essential viewing. It also operates two privately run satellite channels, Al Maghribiya and Mid 1 Sat.

## Money

Only restricted amounts of Moroccan dirhams (DH) can be imported or exported, which means there's a limit on how many you can get hold of in advance of your trip. On departure you can change unspent dirhams back into hard currency at the airport.

The dirham is a reasonably stable currency. Recent exchange rates have hovered around 13.5DH to £1 sterling, 11DH to E1, and 8DH to $1. Rates vary between banks, so shop around.

### ATMs

ATMs are the easiest way of obtaining cash, although your bank may charge you a handling fee as well as interest if you are using a credit card (you can often use debit cards bearing the Cirrus logo, but don't rely on this alone). ATMs are plentiful in the New Town, and there are a couple of Banque Populaire ATMs at the top of Rue Bab Agnaou, off the Jemaa el Fna. The daily limit on withdrawals is usually 2,000DH.

### Credit cards

MasterCard and Visa are accepted in most hotels, petrol stations and the more expensive shops and restaurants. Other cards are less widely accepted.

### Tipping

It is usual to tip porters, chambermaids, other hotel staff if they are particularly helpful, and waiting staff. There are no

*Ben Youssef Madrassa*

hard-and-fast rules for the amount, although 10 percent would be considered generous.

# P

## Police

Most matters concerning tourists are handled by the Tourist Police, who have a station on the northern side of the Jemaa el Fna (tel: 0524-38 46 01). Just threatening to call them is often a good way of getting people who are hassling you to leave you alone.

## Post

The main post office (PTT) is on Place 16 Novembre in Guéliz. Stamps are available from tobacconists.

# R

## Religion

### Islam

Morocco is a comparatively tolerant Muslim country, but religion is still the biggest influence on society. The five requirements of Islam – affirmation that there is no other god but God and Mohammed is his Prophet; prayer five times a day; the observance of Ramadan; the giving of alms to the poor; and making the *hadj* (pilgrimage) to Mecca at least once in a lifetime – are central to many Moroccan lives.

Officially, Morocco follows the Sunni (orthodox) branch of Islam. However, there are many thriving Sufi brotherhoods that promote a more mystical approach to God.

### Christianity

Marrakech has a small Christian community, served by the little Catholic church in Guéliz (see page 55).

### Ramadan

The ninth month of the Muslim calendar was the one in which God revealed to Mohammed the truths that were written as the Qur'an. In remembrance of this and in obedience to one of Islam's 'five pillars', Muslims must observe a fast during the hours of daylight. For travellers and non-Muslims, the unique atmosphere of Ramadan – the festive spirit in the evenings – can be weighed against slight material inconveniences (most cafés and restaurants close during the day). Non-Muslims are not required to observe the fast, but abstinence from smoking, eating and displays of physical affection in public is tactful.

Visiting Marrakech (and, especially, the rural areas around the city) during Ramadan can be both rewarding and tricky, but knowing a few basic rules will help make things much easier. Restaurants and cafés are much quieter during the day (some even close for the month), and some places that normally sell alcohol do not during this time.

Everything tends to shut down around half an hour before the breaking of the fast, at sunset, and it will also be impos-

*Busy market*

sible to find taxis at this time and for about an hour after sunset. Most places catering to tourism will remain open. Be aware that sensitivities can be more pronounced during this sacred month, so dressing and behaving appropriately is important. If you are ever invited to break the fast with a Moroccan, accept – but be prepared for a long night of eating ahead of you.

# S

## Smoking

Smoking is virtually a Moroccan pastime, and there are no restrictions on smoking in restaurants or cafés. For women smokers, however, it is worth bearing in mind that Moroccan women almost never smoke in public.

# T

## Telephones

There are three main licensed telecommunications companies operating in Morocco: Maroc Télécom, Meditel and Inwi. Domestic and international telephone calls can be made from phone boxes (*cabines*) on the street, or in a main post office. Most public telephones now take phone cards rather than cash; cards are available from post offices, tobacco shops and some grocery stores. Private payphone booths (*téléboutiques*) are widespread and efficient; they cost little more than a payphone on the street.

If you want to use your own mobile in Morocco without paying hefty international rates and roaming charges, local SIM cards issued by the major mobile telecoms providers are readily available, offering inexpensive local call rates.

To make an international call, dial 00 for an international line, followed by the country code (44 for the UK). Remember to drop the initial zero of the UK area code you are dialling.

## Time

Moroccan time is the same as Greenwich Mean Time. Daily Saving Time (DST, one hour ahead of GMT) is traditionally used during the summer between roughly late April and early October, although, to confuse matters further, DST is cancelled during the month of Ramadan, when the country reverts to GMT.

## Tourist Information

The main tourist office is on Place Abdel Moumen Ben Ali in Guéliz (tel: 0524-43 61 79). It is open Mon–Fri 8.30am–noon and 2.30–6.30pm, Sat 9am–noon and 3–6pm.

## Tours

There are countless local companies offering a wide range of tours, from short, guided tours in Marrakech to excursions into the Atlas and southern Morocco. Reputable companies include: Morocco Adventure Tours (tel: 0618-96 42 52; www.moroccoadventuretours.

*Kasbah Tamadot*

com), who specialize in outdoor activities and white-water rafting, but also do various other packages including city tours and cookery courses; **Ribat Tours** (First Floor, no. 80 Rue Bab Agnou; tel: 0524-42 98 98; www.ribatours. com), who specialise in outdoor activities; and **Terres et Voyages** (Immeuble D1, 8 Avenue 11 Janvier, Bab Doukkala; tel: 0524-43 71 53; www.terres-etvoyages.com), a reliable mainstream tour operator, with an English-speaking owner.

## Transport

### Arrival by air

Marrakech is well served by international flights and is where the majority of Morocco's tourist visitors arrive. There are direct budget flights here from London with easyJet (from Gatwick; www.easyjet.com), Ryanair (from Luton; www.ryanair.com) and Thomson (from London Gatwick, Manchester, Birmingham and Bristol; www.thomsonfly. com), as well as British Airways (from Heathrow). The city also has good connections on Royal Air Maroc to numerous other European cities.

### Arrival by train

It is possible to reach Marrakech overland via Europe by train via Paris (Eurostar to Gare du Nord and then change to Gare d'Austerlitz) for Algeciras, where ferries leave for Tangier throughout the day. From Tangier there are around nine daytime trains to Marrakech (journey time

9–10 hours), with a change of trains in either Casablanca or Sidi Kacem, but you're best off booking a couchette on the direct overnight train, which leaves daily at 9.35pm and arrives at 8am.

In Tangier you will need to take a taxi from the ferry terminal to the railway station, as they are at opposite ends of the bay. The first-class couchettes accommodate four passengers in each compartment, and, although not luxurious, are comfortable enough. There is normally only one couchette carriage, so it is advisable to book your place well in advance. Latest timetables and fares can be checked at www. oncf.ma.

### Arrival by road

After taking the ferry from Algeciras to Tangier, it is a 600km (370-mile) drive along the modern and wonderfully deserted toll motorway to Marrakech.

### Airport

Upon arrival at **Marrakech's Menara airport** (code RAK; tel: 0524-44 79 10, http://marrakech.airport-authority.com) you will be required to fill out an immigration form before going through passport control.

The arrivals hall has the usual facilities, including a bank and cash machine, and car-hire firms. There are two terminals, although they effectively merge into one (with a third one due to open in 2014/15): terminal 2 handles all of the budget airlines.

*Train station*

On departure you will also need to fill out an immigration form before passing through passport control. The café in the departure lounge will take euros as well as dirhams.

The airport is about 3km (2 miles) southwest of the city. The taxi drivers at the airport here are notoriously crooked. Taxi fares to the centre of town are officially set at an already steep 70DH, or 100DH to outlying areas like the Palmeraie (with a 50 percent increase from 9pm to 6am), although drivers may try for anything up to 200DH. Always agree the fare before getting in. A shuttle bus (20DH) also runs between the airport and Jemaa el Fna, departing every 30min between around 6am and 9pm. Alternatively, local bus no. 11 runs every 20–30min to the Jemaa el Fna.

## Transport within Marrakech

**Taxis.** There are two types of taxi in Morocco: *petits taxis* (greeny-beige livery in Marrakech) and *grands taxis* (large cream Mercedes).

**Petits taxis** take up to four passengers and can be hired on the street. Fares are cheap, but drivers usually refuse to use the meter so you'll need to agree a fare before you set off. It is not unusual for people to share *petits taxis*, so don't be surprised if your driver picks up another passenger along the way.

**Grands taxis** rattle along with up to six passengers on routes from town to town, charging a fixed price. They leave when they are full. The fares are a bit higher than the bus, but the journey is always quicker. You can charter a *grand taxi* for the day or for a longer trip (easily arranged through your hotel, or more cheaply by negotiating directly with drivers at the *grands-taxis* stations; make sure you know the going rate). In Guéliz the main station is next door to the train station on Avenue Hassan II.

**City buses.** There is a good bus service, although buses can get very crowded. One of the most useful buses for tourists is the no. 1 from Place de Foucauld to Place Abdel Moumen Ben Ali. Other useful routes are nos 2 and 10 for the bus station, and nos 3 and 8 for the train station. The flat fare on all buses is 3.5DH. Payment is made upon boarding; drivers will supply change for smaller notes.

**Calèches.** Horse-drawn carriages congregate outside the larger hotels and at various points around the city, most notably opposite Club Med on Place de Foucauld. Official prices are posted inside the calèche but it's very unlikely the driver will stick to them and you'll need to barter (hard) for a fare before you set off – aim for something in the region of 150DH per hour.

**Trains.** The entrance to Marrakech's train station is on Avenue Mohammed VI. The station runs direct services to Casablanca, Rabat, Fez, Tangier and Meknès. First-class carriages have the advantage of being air-conditioned and

*Marrakech's airport*

less crowded – on popular routes and at busy times, travelling first-class is the only way to guarantee getting a seat. For information: tel: 090-20 30 40; www.oncf.ma.

**Long-distance bus/coach travel.** Supratours (tel: 0524-47 53 17; www.supratourstravel.com) and CTM (tel: 0524-43 44 02; www.ctm.ma) are the most useful companies; their buses are comfortable and reasonably priced (about 20 percent cheaper than the train). The Supratours office is on Avenue Hassan II, next door to the *grands taxis* and railway stations.

## Visas and passports

Holders of full British passports or American passports can enter Morocco for a stay of up to three months without a visa, but their passport must be valid for at least six months after the planned departure date.

## Websites

www.visitmorocco.com Website of the national tourist office
www.maroc.net News, culture and useful information.
www.terremaroc.com Tourist information site. Particularly good for finding riad accommodation.
www.morocco.com Includes hotel booking and travel tips.

www.hipmarrakech.com Good list of riads and a restaurant guide.
www.ilovemarrakech.com Online travel guide.
www.bestrestaurantsmaroc.com Restaurant listings
www.morocco-holidays-guide.co.uk Listings (sites, hotels) for the major cities.
www.moroccanfood.about.com Moroccan recipes galore
www.madein-marrakech.com The best general city website, with listings galore, comprehensive details of latest events and lots of other information

## Women travellers

Women travelling alone or with female friends often complain of unwanted attention from Moroccan men – although contrary to popular belief, Western women are no more likely to attract attention of this nature than Moroccan women.

Although this is hard to avoid completely, a few simple common sense measures should help to keep the problem to a minimum. Dressing modestly is the most important of these. Short (above-the-knee) skirts or shorts and vest tops are best left at home (although they're acceptable on the beach).

Assuming a confident manner on the streets can help deter all but the most persistent males. Keep hassle to a minimum by behaving coolly but courteously, wearing modest clothing and avoiding eye contact and entering into conversation.

*Avenue Mohammed VI sign*

# LANGUAGE

The official language in Morocco is Arabic. Moroccans speak *darija*, their own dialect, but written communication is in standard, modern Arabic. The Berbers speak various dialects of their own. Although most Berbers now speak and understand Arabic, few Arabs understand Berber.

French is widely spoken and understood, although fluency is not as widespread as it once was. In tourist areas, you will be surprised by youngsters speaking several languages. Here are some helpful phrases in Moroccan-dialect Arabic and French.

## Useful phrases

**Hello, how are you?** *Márhaba, la bes?* Bonjour, ça va?

**reply** *Bikheer? Bonjour*

**Greetings (formal)** *As-salám aláykum*

**reply** *Waláykum as-salam*

**Welcome** *Márhaba* Soyez le bienvenu

**Good morning** *Sabáh el-kháyr* Bonjour

**Good evening** *Mesá el-kháyr* Bonsoir

**Goodbye** *Bessaláma* Au revoir

**How are you?** *La bes/Káyf hálak (to m)/Káyf hálik (to f)?* Ça va?

**Fine, thank you** *Bikheer el-hámdu li-lláh* Ça va, merci

**Please** *'Afak, 'afik, 'afakum (to m, f, pl)* S'il vous plaît

**Thank you (very much)** *Shúkran (bez-zef)* Merci (beaucoup)

**Thanks be to God** *El-hámdu li-lláh*

**Yes** *Eeyeh/náam* Oui

**No** *La* Non

**If God wills** *Insha'allah?* Si Dieu le veut

**What is your name?** *Asmeetek?* C'est quoi votre nom?

**My name is...** *Esmee...* Je m'appelle

**Where are you from?** *Mneen enta/enti/entum? (to m/f/pl)* Vous êtes d'où?

**I am from England/the United States** *Ana min Inglaterra/Amrika* Je suis anglais(e) /américain(e)

**Do you speak English/French?** *Wash kat'ref negleezeeya/faranseeya?* Vous parlez anglais/français?

**I do not understand** *Mafhemtsh* Je ne comprends pas

**I understand** *Fhemt* Je comprends

**What does this mean?** *Ash kat'anee hadhee?* Qu'est-ce que ça veut dire?

**Never mind** *Makain mushkil* Pas de problème

**It is forbidden** *Mamnú'* C'est interdit

## Time

**What time is it?** *Shal fessa'a?* Il est quelle heure?

**When?** *Emta/Fuqash?* Quand?

**Today** *Elyaum* Aujourd'hui

**Tomorrow** *Ghedda* Demain

**Yesterday** *Lbareh* Hier

**Morning** *Fi-ssbah* Le matin

**Afternoon/evening** *Fil-sheeya* L'après-midi/le soir

*Cyclists in the mountains*

## Eating/drinking

**coffee/tea** *áhwa/shái* café/thé
**with milk** *wa hleb* au lait
**with/without sugar** *wa/bla sukur* avec/ sans sucre
**with mint** *b'na'na'* à la menthe
**mineral water** *mái ma'adaniya* une eau minérale
**I am a vegetarian** *Ana nabbáti (for m)/ nabbatiya (for f)* Je suis végétarien(ne)
**the bill please** *el-hsáb 'afek* L'addition, s'il vous plaît

## Shopping

**market** *souk* le marché
**money** *flóos* l'argent
**I want to change money** *Bgheet nser- ref floos* Je veux changer de l'argent
**How much is it?** *Bshhal?* C'est com- bien?
**It's too expensive** *Ghalee bezzef* C'est trop cher

## Accommodation

**How much does a room cost per night?** *Bash halkayn gbayt i wahed leyla?* La chambre est à combien la nuit?
**I would like a room...** *Bgheet shee beet...* Je voudrais une chambre...
**for one person** *dyal wahed* pour une personne
**for two people** *dyal jooj* double
**with a bathroom** *belhammam* avec salle de bain
**shower** *dúsh* douche
**air conditioning** *kleemateezaseeyun* climatisation

## Emergencies

**Help** *'Teqnee!* Au secours!
**doctor** *tbeeb* médecin
**hospital** *mustáshfa* hôpital
**pharmacy** *saidalíya* pharmacie
**I am sick** *Ana mreed/mreeda (f)* Je suis malade
**police** *esshúrta* la police

## Transport

**Where..?** *Feen?* Où?
**taxi** *ettaks* le taxi
**train station** *lagaar* la gare
**bus station** *mehetta dyal uttubisaat* la gare routière
**airport** *elmataar* l'aéroport
**to** *li/íla* à
**from** *min* de
**right** *leemen* à droite
**left** *leeser* à gauche
**How far..?** *Bsshal ba'yd?* Est-ce que c'est loin...?

## Numbers

**0** *sifr* zero
**1** *wahed* un/une
**2** *jooj* deux
**3** *Kleta* trois
**4** *Arb'a* quatre
**5** *khamsa* cinq
**6** *setta* six
**7** *sab'a* sept
**8** *tmenya* huit
**9** *tes'ood* neuf
**10** *ashra* dix
**20** *ishreen* vingt
**30** *Kleteen* trente
**100** *miya* cent

# BOOKS AND FILM

Every night in the Jemaa el Fna, storytellers retell the tales of old heroes, of desperate love and of the glorious city of Marrakech. Morocco has a long tradition of poetry and stories, passed on orally for the simple reason that for years most people could not read.

Marrakech has inspired foreign writers too. The Beat writers of the 1950s and 1960s were fascinated by the old stories, and added a few of their own; some ventured to Marrakech on their travels and, in the process, influenced a generation of Moroccan authors.

Foreign filmmakers have been similarly besotted with Marrakech and its surroundings over the years, and just about any Hollywood film in need of an ancient, biblical or Middle Eastern set is filmed in Morocco. Many films are shot at the Atlas Film Studios in Ouarzazate (which can be visited; see page 86), while the fortified village of Ait-Benhaddou (see page 86) is kept in excellent condition due to the number of Hollywood movies filmed here.

Cinema in Morocco has been boosted by current, movie-loving King Mohammed VI, who has made the Marrakech Film Festival into a well-regarded international event, while promoting the country as the place to film blockbusters.

## Books

### Novels

***This Blinding Absence of Light***. Tahar Ben Jelloun. Based on the true story of a political prisoner who survived incarceration in an underground prison in the Moroccan desert for 20 years under the brutal regime of Hassan II.

***Hideous Kinky***. Esther Freud. Novel based on the author's experience of living in Marrakech with her sister and hippie mother in the 1960s. Later turned into a film, set in the 1970s, starring Kate Winslet.

***The Sheltering Sky***. Paul Bowles. The story of a couple descending into darkness and madness in the Moroccan desert. Also a film.

### History and society

***The Last Storytellers***. Richard Hamilton. Collection of folktales handed down by the Jemaa el Fna storytellers.

***Lords of the Atlas***. Gavin Maxwell. Compelling story of the Glaoui dynasty that lorded over Marrakech and most of the High Atlas before and during the era of the French Protectorate.

### Travel literature

***Cinema Eden***. Juan Goytisolo. Stories about Marrakech and other Moroccan places by this Spanish writer fascinated by rituals, traditions and stories.

***Marrakesh (Through Writers' Eyes).*** Ed. Barnaby Rogerson. Compendium of literary extracts from writers ranging from Elias Canetti to Edith Wharton.

***Morocco: The Traveller's Companion.*** Margaret and Robert Bidwell. Literary guide to Morocco, bringing together a range of travel writing on the country.

***Valley of the Casbahs.*** Jeffrey Tayler. Fascinating account of Tayler's journey along the Drâa Valley by foot and camel.

***Voices of Marrakesh.*** Elias Canetti. Lyrical impressions of the city by Nobel Prize-winner.

***A Year in Marrakesh.*** Peter Mayne. Engaging account of the author's stay in the city during the early 1950s.

## Films

### Moroccan films

***Marock*** (2005). Leila Marrakchi's tender love story between a Jewish boy and a Muslim girl.

***Mémoires en Détention*** *(Memories in Detention;* 2004*).* Jilali Ferhati's very realistic account of an ex-prisoner trying to find the relations of a friend who loses his memory in prison.

***Mille Mois*** *(A Thousands Months;* 2003*).* Faouz Bensaïdi's film follows the everyday life of a family in a small town in Morocco during Ramadan.

***Les Yeux Secs*** *(Cry No More;* 2003*).* The story of a former prostitute returning to her village to save her daughter from repeating her mistakes.

### Western films

***Hideous Kinky*** (1998). Based in Esther Freud's book (see page 136), this film follows Gillies MacKinnon to the hippie Marrakech of the 1970s.

***Jesus of Nazareth*** (1977). Franco Zeffirelli's controversial biopic of the Son of God, shot in and around Aït Benhaddou, which was substantially restored and rebuilt during filming.

***The Last Temptation of Christ*** (1988). Martin Scorsese's inflammatory movie, shot entirely in Marrakech

***Lawrence of Arabia*** (1962). David Lean's classic, based on the life of T.E. Lawrence and starring Peter O'Toole, was partly filmed around Ouarzazate.

***The Man Who Knew Too Much (1956).*** Alfred Hitchcock's second version of this thriller was partly shot in Marrakech.

***The Man Who Would be King*** (1975). John Huston's classic Kipling adaptation, starring Michael Caine, Sean Connery and Christopher Plummer, was shot in the Atlas Mountains.

***The Mummy*** (1999). Rip-roaring adventure with Marrakech and the Moroccan Sahara standing in for the tombs and deserts of Egypt.

***Othello*** (1948). Orson Welles' classic, shot in Essaouira (then still known as Mogador), because Welles wanted to return Shakespeare's Moor to his homeland.

***The Sheltering Sky*** (1990). Bernardo Bertolucci's acclaimed film adaptation of Paul Bowles' classic novel. Stars John Malkovich and Debra Winger.

# ABOUT THIS BOOK

This *Explore Guide* has been produced by the editors of Insight Guides, whose books have set the standard for visual travel guides since 1970. With top-quality photography and authoritative recommendations, these guidebooks bring you the very best routes and itineraries in the world's most exciting destinations.

## BEST ROUTES

The routes in the book provide something to suit all budgets, tastes and trip lengths. As well as covering the destination's many classic attractions, the itineraries track lesser-known sights, and there are also excursions for those who want to extend their visit outside the city. The routes embrace a range of interests, so whether you are an art fan, a gourmet, a history buff or have kids to entertain, you will find an option to suit.

We recommend reading the whole of a route before setting out. This should help you to familiarise yourself with it and enable you to plan where to stop for refreshments – options are shown in the 'Food and Drink' box at the end of each tour.

For our pick of the tours by theme, consult Recommended Routes for… (see pages 4–5).

## INTRODUCTION

The routes are set in context by this introductory section, giving an overview of the destination to set the scene, plus background information on food and drink, shopping and more, while a succinct history timeline highlights the key events over the centuries.

## DIRECTORY

Also supporting the routes is a Directory chapter, with a clearly organised A–Z of practical information, our pick of where to stay while you are there and select restaurant listings; these eateries complement the more low-key cafés and restaurants that feature within the routes and are intended to offer a wider choice for evening dining. Also included here are some nightlife listings, plus a handy language guide and our recommendations for books and films about the destination.

## ABOUT THE AUTHORS

This Explore guide was worked on by regular Insight contributor Gavin Thomas, a freelance travel writer specializing in Asia and Arabia who has also contributed to numerous other Insight guides including books on Morocco, Oman, Dubai and the UAE, Sri Lanka and India. A regular visitor to Morocco for over 15 years, he has now travelled through most of the country from the mountains of the Rif to the southern Saharan oases but always seems to end up back in Marrakech in time for dinner on the Jemaa el Fna.

This book builds on original content by Dorothy Stannard and Charlie Shepherd.

## CONTACT THE EDITORS

We hope you find this Explore Guide useful, interesting and a pleasure to read. If you have any questions or feedback on the text, pictures or maps, please do let us know. If you have noticed any errors or outdated facts, or have suggestions for places to include on the routes, we would be delighted to hear from you. Please drop us an email at insight@apaguide.co.uk. Thanks!

# CREDITS

**Explore Marrakech**
**Contributors:** Gavin Thomas
**Commissioning Editor:** Tom Stainer
**Series Editor:** Sarah Clark
**Pictures/Art:** Tom Smyth/Shahid Mahmood
**Map Production:** originial cartography
Geographic, updated by Apa Cartography
Department
**Production:** Rebeka Davies
**Photo credits:** Alamy 5MR, 24, 40, 42/43,
45R, 60, 64, 92, 120/121; Clay Perry/Apa
Publications 2ML, 2MC, 2MR, 2MC, 2ML,
2/3T, 4TL, 4BC, 5T, 5MR, 5M, 6ML, 6ML,
6MC, 6MR, 6/7T, 8, 9L, 10, 10/11, 13R,
14, 17R, 18, 19, 22, 28MC, 28MR, 28MR,
28/29T, 30, 31L, 32, 32/33, 33R, 34/35,
37, 41, 43R, 44, 44/45, 49, 50, 50/51,
54, 55, 61, 63, 65R, 68, 70, 71R, 70/71,
72, 73, 74, 75, 76, 77, 78, 79, 81R, 80/81,
82, 84, 84/85, 90, 93, 94, 94/95, 95R,
96/97, 97R, 98ML, 98MR, 98ML, 98/99T,
100, 101, 104, 104/105, 105R, 106, 107,
109, 111, 114, 122, 129, 135; Corbis
80; Dreamstime 1, 12/13, 22/23, 53R,
52/53, 62, 66/67, 69, 86/87, 108, 136;
Getty Images 51R; iStockphoto 8/9, 11R,
25, 30/31, 42, 48, 85R, 91; Mary Evans
Picture Library 26, 27; Ming Tang-Evans/
Apa Publications 2MR, 4MC, 4ML, 6MC,
6MR, 12, 15, 16, 16/17, 20, 20/21, 21R,
23R, 28ML, 28ML, 28MC, 34, 35L, 36,
38, 38/39, 39R, 46, 46/47, 47R, 52,
56, 57, 58, 59, 64/65, 83, 86, 87R, 88,
88/89, 89R, 96, 98MC, 98MR, 98MC, 102,
102/103, 103R, 110, 112, 113, 114/115,
115R, 116, 117, 118, 118/119, 119R,
123, 124, 124/125, 125R, 126, 126/127,
127R, 128, 130, 131, 132, 133, 134, 137
**Cover credits:** Front Cover Main: Mamounia
Hotel, *4Corners Images*; Front Cover BL:
Spice Square, *Ming Tang-Evans/Apa Publications*; Back Cover: (Left) Jemaa El Fna,
*Clay Perry/Apa Publications*; (Right): Sand
dunes at Tinfou, *Clay Perry/Apa Publications*

Printed by CTPS – China
© 2014 Apa Publications (UK) Ltd
All Rights Reserved

First Edition 2014

## DISTRIBUTION

**Worldwide**
APA Publications GmbH & Co. Verlag KG
(Singapore branch)
7030 Ang Mo Kio Ave 5, 08-65
Northstar @ AMK, Singapore 569880
Email: apasin@singnet.com.sg
**UK and Ireland**
Dorling Kindersley Ltd (a Penguin Company)
80 Strand, London, WC2R 0RL, UK
Email: sales@uk.dk.com
**US**
Ingram Publisher Services
One Ingram Blvd, PO Box 3006, La Vergne,
TN 37086-1986
Email: ips@ingramcontent.com
**Australia and New Zealand**
Woodslane
10 Apollo St, Warriewood NSW 2102,
Australia
Email: info@woodslane.com.au

# INDEX